Pocket PCT

Complete Data and Town Guide
to the Pacific Crest Trail

Fourth Edition

by Paul Bodnar

Pocket PCT

Complete Data and Town Guide to the Pacific Crest Trail

Copyright © 2016
Paul Bodnar, High Sierra Attitude, LLC
sierraattitude.com

Cover Photo:
South Sisters in Oregon
Photo by Ryan "The Tourist" Choi
Pictured left to right: "Wildflower", "Nips" and "Beef Nuggets"

Safety Notice: Trail conditions change. Check local conditions prior to hiking. Always carry a detailed map and compass while hiking. The author is not responsible for any loss, damage or injury that may occur to anyone using this book.

Introduction

The Pocket PCT contains an elevation profile and important landmarks on the Pacific Crest Trail (PCT). Each chapter begins and ends at a common resupply location. The elevation profile is broken into ten-mile segments, showing the trail's elevation in feet. Water sources, landmarks, roads and trails are indicated above the elevation profile line. Additional important town information is also provided.

A SPECIAL WARNING ABOUT WATER: always develop a water resupply plan and check current trail conditions prior to your hike. I also recommend marking this book with your own notes on water and other landmarks.

CHECK POCKETPCT.COM FOR UPDATES

Happy Hiking,

Paul

My Wife Alice is the Bestest

Symbols & Abbreviations

Ⓡ Full Resupply Point
®̲ Marginal Resupply Point
Ⓡ Minimal Resupply Point
🌢 Reliable Water Source
◔ Marginal Water Source
◌ Unreliable Water Source
▮ Possible Water Cache
• Landmark
! Water Warning (Limited Water Ahead)
▲ Campground
△ Tentsite (number of sites)
╪ Powerlines
⌒ Bridge
⊟ Gate or Fence
▢ Dirt Road
▪ Paved Road
⊦ Junction

NB Northbound on the PCT
SB Southbound on the PCT
CG Campground
TH Trailhead
Ck. Creek
Jct. Junction
Lk. Lake
m mile
Mtn. Mountain
R. River
Rd. Road
Spg. Spring
Mdw. Meadow
BB Bear Box

Water source ratings may not reflect current conditions. Always treat water prior to consumption.

Symbols & Abbreviations

Ⓡ **Full Resupply Point** indicates a place where a grocery store can be found. A hiker can easily resupply from these stores. Resupply package pickup available.

Ⓡ **Marginal Resupply Point** indicates a large convenience store or small grocery store. A hiker could potentially resupply from these stores, however selection is very limited. Resupply package pickup available.

Ⓡ **Minimum Resupply Point** indicates a place where only snacks can be purchased. A hiker could not be expected to resupply from these stores. Resupply package pickup available.

🌢 **Reliable Water Source** indicates a high likelihood of water. Water is commonly reported at these locations.

🌢 **Marginal or Seasonal Water Source** indicates a probability of water. Water may or may not be located here. Water at these locations is dependent on the season, weather and other factors.

🌢 **Unreliable Water Source** indicates an unlikely source of water. Water is rarely reported in these locations.

Town Symbols

✉ Package Service	@ Internet
🛏 Lodging	Sporting Goods
⛺ Camping	Hardware Store
🛒 Grocery Store	Restroom
Small Market	Shower
🍴 Restaurant	ATM ATM
Laundry Services	Transportation
Library	Movie Theater

Table of Contents

CALIFORNIA

OREGON

WASHINGTON

In every walk with nature one receives far more than he seeks.

John Muir

Mexico to Mt. Laguna

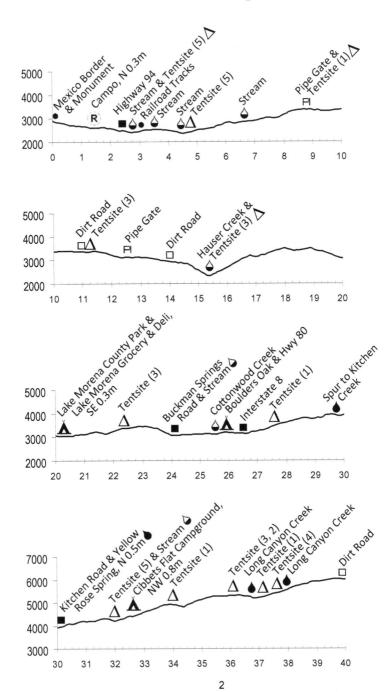

Mexico to Mt. Laguna

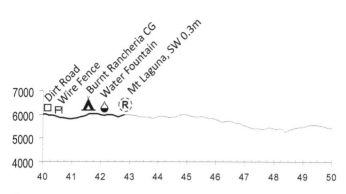

Campo   Mile 1 N 0.3 miles   Population: 2,684

U.S. Post Office, 619-478-5466, M-F 8:30-11:30 12:30-4:30, Sa 9:30-12
Campo, CA 91906

Tip: Visit the PCT Facebook group to learn more about transportation to the border.

Mount Laguna   Mile 43 SW 0.3 miles   Population: 57

U.S. Post Office, 619-473-8341, M-F 12-4, Sa 9-11
Mt. Laguna, CA 91948

Laguna Mountain Lodge Open daily 9-5, $Fee per box
619-473-8533, visit lagunamountain.com for details.

UPS	US Mail
c/o Laguna Mountain Lodge	**c/o Laguna Mountain Lodge**
10678 Sunrise Hwy	**P.O. Box 146**
Mount Laguna, CA 91948	**Mount Laguna, CA 91948**

Tip: Coin showers are located at the Burnt Ranchero Campground

Cost Saving Tip: Consider buying the Guthook's PCT Guide app available for the iPhone and Android. This app will help you stay on trail and save time in town. Learn more at pocketpct.com.

CHECK POCKETPCT.COM FOR UPDATES

Mt. Laguna to Warner Springs

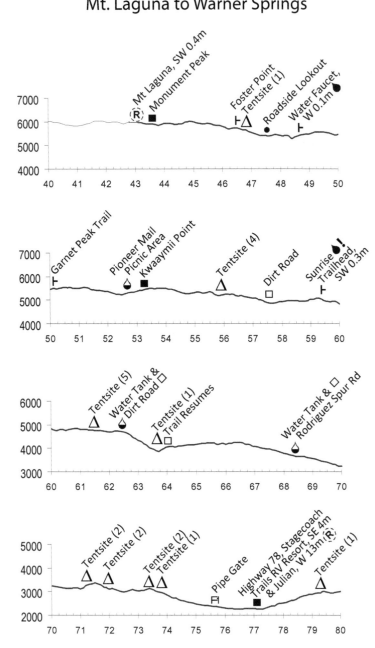

Mt. Laguna to Warner Springs

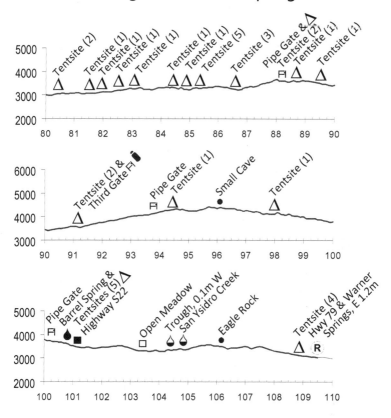

Mount Laguna   Mile 43 SW 0.3 miles   Population: 57

U.S. Post Office, 619-473-8341, M-F 12-4, Sa 9-11
Mt. Laguna, CA 91948

Laguna Mountain Lodge Open daily 9-5, $Fee per box
619-473-8533, visit lagunamountain.com for details.

UPS   US Mail
**c/o Laguna Mountain Lodge   c/o Laguna Mountain Lodge
10678 Sunrise Hwy   P.O. Box 146
Mount Laguna, CA 91948   Mount Laguna, CA 91948**

Tip: Coin showers are located at the Burnt Ranchero
Campground

CHECK POCKETPCT.COM FOR UPDATES

Mt. Laguna to Warner Springs

Julian   Mile 77 W 13 miles   Population: 1,502

U.S. Post Office, 760-765-3648, M-F 9-4, Sa 10-12
Julian, CA 92036

Tip: Mom's Pies gives a free slice of pie to PCT hikers.

Stagecoach RV Park   Mile 77 SE 4 miles   Population: 0

Visit stagecoachtrails.com for details. 760-765-3765

Tip: Stagecoach RV Park is located SE 4 miles on Hwy S2.
The RV Park has tenting, pool, laundry, showers and a deli.

Warner Springs   Mile 109 E 1.2 mile   Population: 1,191

U.S. Post Office, 760-782-3166, M-F 8-11, 11:30-4, Sa 8-1:30
Warner Springs, CA 92086

Tip: The Warner Springs Community Center is located
near the PCT on Hwy 79. It offers camping, showers, laundry,
limited supplies and food. Warner Springs Ranch Resort is
scheduled to fully open in 2016/2017.

Cost Saving Tip: Staying at an RV park instead of a motel can
save you a lot of money. Most RV parks along the PCT
provide showers, laundry, internet and tenting.

Warner Springs to Idyllwild

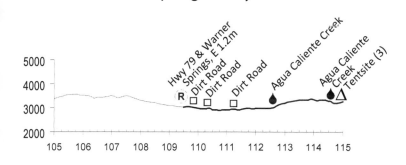

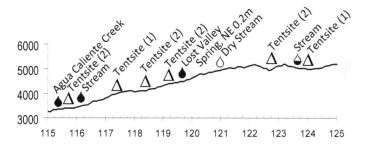

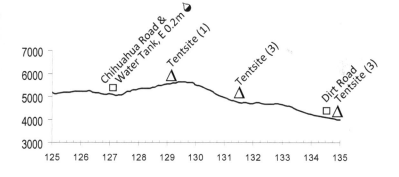

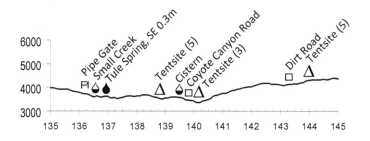

Warner Springs to Idyllwild

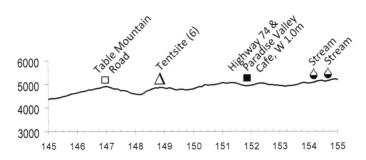

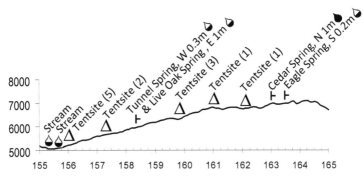

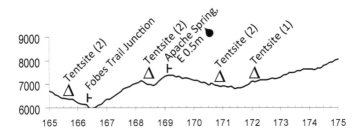

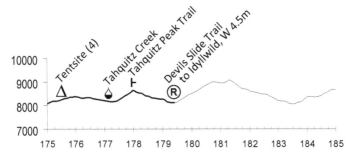

Warner Springs to Idyllwild

Warner Springs   Mile 109 E 1.2 mile   Population: 1,191

U.S. Post Office, 760-782-3166, M-F 8-11, 11:30-4, Sa 8-1:30
Warner Springs, CA 92086

Tip: The Warner Springs Community Center is located
near the PCT on Hwy 79. It offers camping, showers, laundry,
limited supplies and food. Warner Springs Ranch Resort is
scheduled to fully open in 2016/2017.

Paradise Valley Cafe   Mile 152 W 1.0 mile   Population: 0

UPS, Fed Ex, USMail, 951-659-3663, Days and times vary,
Visit theparadisevalleycafe.com for details.
c/o Paradise Valley Cafe
61721 Hwy 74
Mountain Center, CA 92561

Tip: Paradise Valley Cafe sometimes closes early on Monday and
Tuesday. Check theparadisevalleycafe.com for hours of service.

Lake Hemet   Mile 152 W 10.2 miles   Population: 0

Tip: Coin Showers are located in the campground.

Idyllwild   Mile 179 W 4.5 miles   Population: 3,874

U.S. Post Office, 951-659-9719, M-F 9-5 & Sa pickup 1:30-3
Idyllwild, CA 92549

Visit idyllwildinn.com for package mailing details.

Tip: La Casita offers $0.99 tacos on Monday & Thursday
night (5-7 PM). Many local restaurants provide discounts
to PCT hikers, so remember to ask.

Cost Saving Tip: Mount San Jacinto State Park in
Idyllwild has affordable backpacker sites.

CHECK POCKETPCT.COM FOR UPDATES

Idyllwild to Big Bear

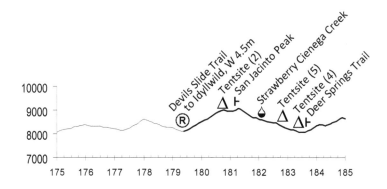

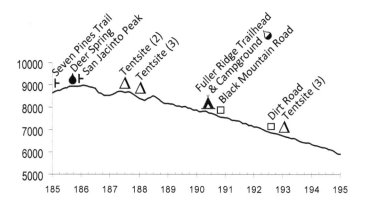

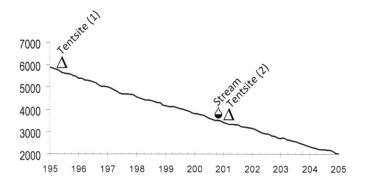

Idyllwild to Big Bear

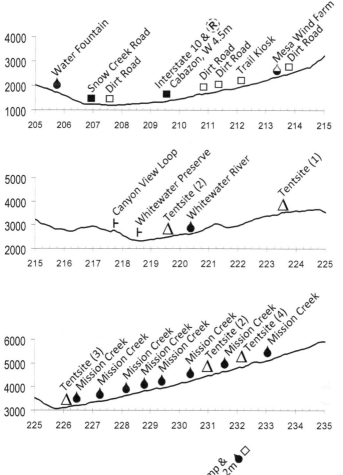

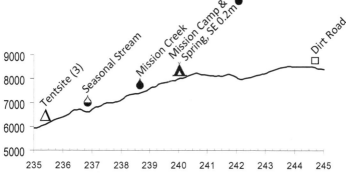

Idyllwild to Big Bear

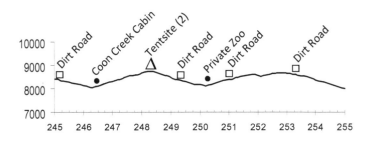

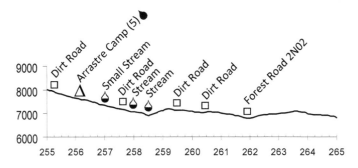

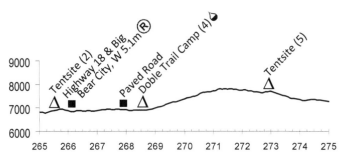

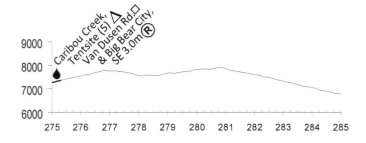

Idyllwild to Big Bear

Idyllwild   Mile 179 W 4.5 miles Population: 3,874

U.S. Post Office, 951-659-9719, M-F 9-5 & Sa pickup 1:30-3
Idyllwild, CA 92549

Visit idyllwildinn.com for package mailing details.

Tip: La Casita offers $0.99 tacos on Monday & Thursday
night (5-7 PM). Many local restaurants provide discounts
to PCT hikers, so remember to ask.

Cabazon   Mile 209 W 4.5 miles   Population: 2,535

U.S. Post Office, 951-849-6233, M-F 8:30-11:30, 12:45-4
Cabazon, CA 92230

Tip: Check out whitewatertrailhouse.com for trail angel and
possible package mailing details.

Big Bear City   Mile 266 W 5.1 miles Population: 12,304
Mile 275 SE 3.5 miles

U.S. Post Office, 909-585-7132, M-F 9-4:30
Big Bear City, CA 92314

Tip: Use the low-cost local shuttle bus for easy transportation.

Big Bear Lake   Mile 266 W 8 miles Population: 5,124
Mile 275 SE 3.5m + W 4.5m

U.S. Post Office, 909-585-7132, M-F 8:30-5, Sa 10-12
Big Bear Lake, CA 92315

Visit bigbearhostel.com for additional details
c/o Big Bear Hostel
P.O. Box 1951
Big Bear Lake, CA 92315-1951

Tip: Check out the International Travelers House hostel at
www.ithhostels.com. It is located close to the "Village".

Cost Saving Tip: Save on postage by buying food in town.

CHECK POCKETPCT.COM FOR UPDATES

Big Bear to Wrightwood

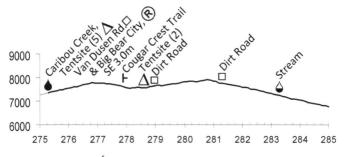

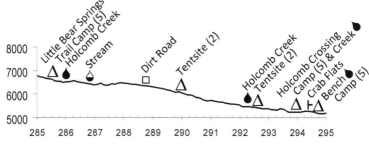

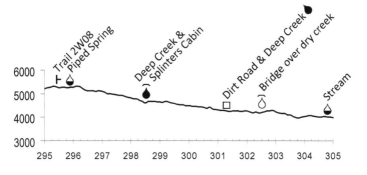

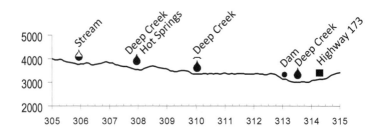

Big Bear to Wrightwood

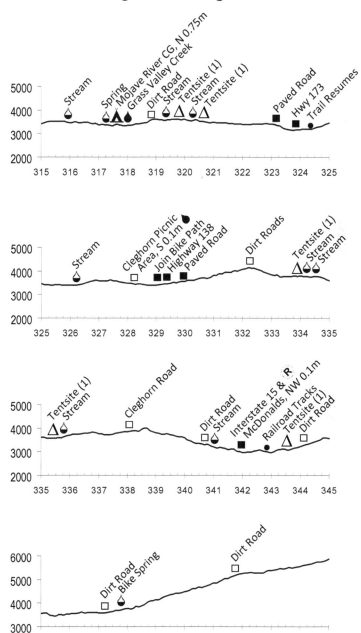

Big Bear to Wrightwood

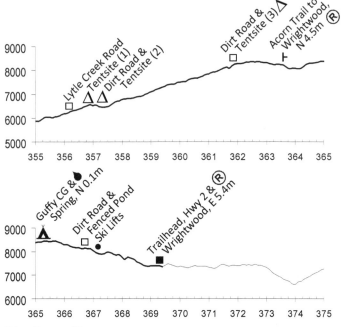

Big Bear City   Mile 266 W 5.1 miles   Population: 12,304
Mile 275 SE 3.5 miles

U.S. Post Office, 909-585-7132, M-F 9-4:30 & Sa pickup 1-2
Big Bear City, CA 92314

Tip: Use the low cost local shuttle bus for easy transportation.

Big Bear Lake   Mile 266 W 8 miles   Population: 5,124
Mile 275 SE 3.5m + W 4.5m

U.S. Post Office, 909-585-7132, M-F 8:30-5, Sa 10-12
Big Bear Lake, CA 92315

Visit bigbearhostel.com for additional details
c/o Big Bear Hostel
P.O. Box 1951
Big Bear Lake, CA 92315-1951

Tip: Check out International Travelers House www.ithhostels.com.

CHECK POCKETPCT.COM FOR UPDATES

Big Bear to Wrightwood

Cajon Pass   Mile 342 NW 0.6 miles   Population: 0

US Mail, 760-249-6777, Hotel open daily with extended hours
c/o Best Western Cajon Pass
8317 US Hwy 138
At the I-15 Freeway
Phelan, CA 92371

Tip: McDonald's is located near the PCT. The Best Western has a hot tub.

Wrightwood   Mile 369 E 5.4 miles   Population: 4,525

U.S. Post Office, 760-249-8882, M-F 8:45-5 & Sa pickup 8-11
Wrightwood, CA 92397

Mountain Hardware, 760-249-3653
Visit mtnhardware.com for additional details.
USMail   UPS
c/o Mountain Hardware   c/o Mountain Hardware
P.O. Box 398   1390 Hwy 2
Wrightwood, CA 92397   Wrightwood, CA 92397

Tip: The hardware store is well stocked for hikers and has a trail register with a list of trail angels.

Cost Saving Tip: Splitting a large pizza is usually better than buying two smaller pizzas. A large pizza is usually 50% cheaper than a smaller pizza when considering the cost per calories.

Wrightwood to Agua Dulce

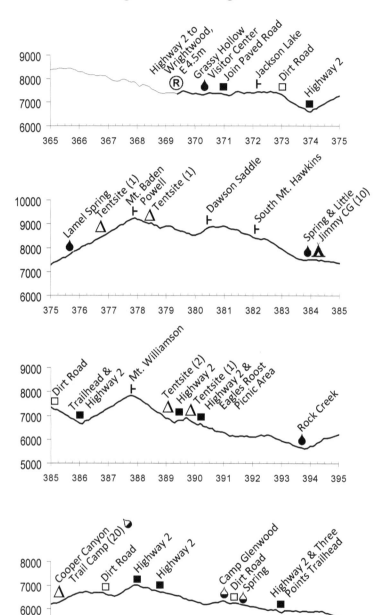

Wrightwood to Agua Dulce

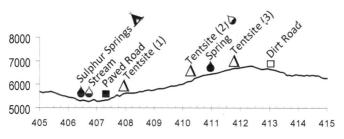

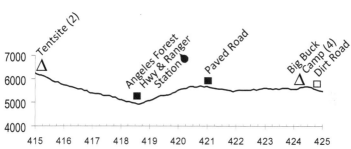

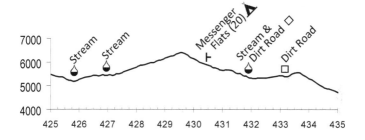

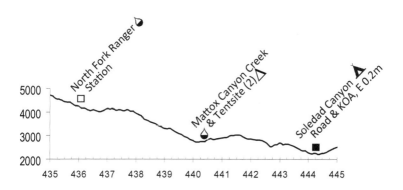

Wrightwood to Agua Dulce

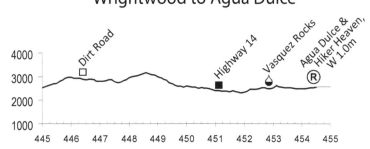

 Dirt Road

 Highway 14

 Vasquez Rocks

Agua Dulce & Hiker Heaven, W 1.0m

Wrightwood   Mile 369 E 5.4 miles   Population: 4,525

U.S. Post Office, 760-249-8882, M-F 8:45-5 & Sa pickup 8-11
Wrightwood, CA 92397

Mountain Hardware, 760-249-3653
Visit mtnhardware.com for additional details.

USMail	UPS
c/o Mountain Hardware	**c/o Mountain Hardware**
P.O. Box 398	**1390 Hwy 2**
Wrightwood, CA 92397	**Wrightwood, CA 92397**

Tip: The hardware store is well stocked for hikers and has a
trail register with a list of trail angels.

KOA   Mile 444 E 0.2 miles   Population: 0

Visit koa.com/campgrounds/acton/ for current details.

Tip: The KOA has a pool.

Agua Dulce   Mile 454 On Trail   Population: 3,342

Visit hikerheaven.com for details.
c/o The Saufleys
11861 Darling Road
Agua Dulce, CA 91390

Tip: Arrive at Hiker Heaven early in the morning to
increase your odds of getting a spot.

Cost Saving Tip: Consider buying stove fuel along the way.
This will save shipping costs and avoid over-purchasing fuel.

CHECK POCKETPCT.COM FOR UPDATES

20

Agua Dulce to Tehachapi

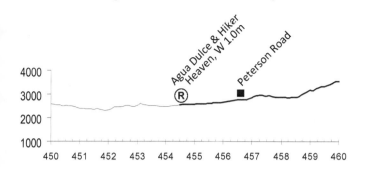

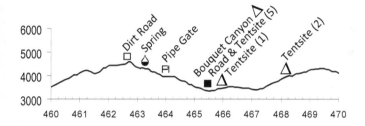

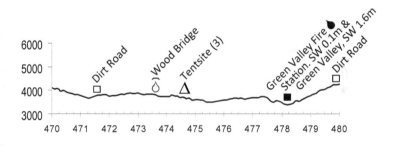

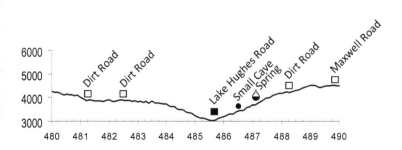

Agua Dulce to Tehachapi

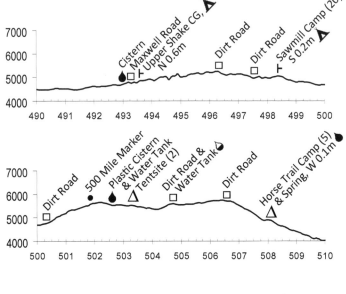

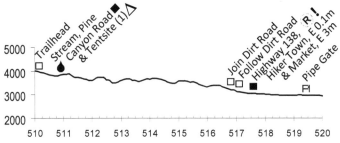

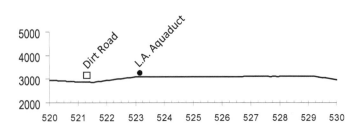

Agua Dulce to Tehachapi

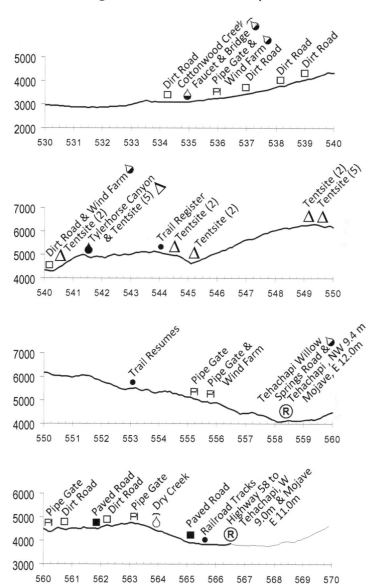

Agua Dulce to Tehachapi

Agua Dulce   Mile 454 On Trail Population: 3,342

Visit hikerheaven.com for details
c/o The Saufleys
11861 Darling Road
Agua Dulce, CA 91390

Tip: Arrive at Hiker Heaven early in the morning to increase your odds of getting a spot.

Green Valley   Mile 478 SW 1.6 miles   Population: 1,625

Tip: If you like to have fun, visit Casa de Luna.

Hikertown   Mile 517 E 0.1miles Population: 2

Visit hikertown.com for details. $Fee per box
c/o Hikertown
26803 W. Ave C-15
Lancaster, CA 93536

Tip: Fairmount Market is located 4 miles to the east. Hikertown offers rides to the market.

Mojave   Mile 566 E 11 miles   Population: 4,238

U.S. Post Office, 661-824-3502, M-F 9-1, 2-4
Mojave, CA 93501

Tip: Call Kern Regional Transit at 800-323-2396 to schedule bus pickup from the Highway 58 overpass to Mojave or Tehachapi.

Tehachapi   Mile 566 W 9 miles   Population: 13,258

U.S. Post Office, 661-822-0279, M-F 9-5, Sa 10-2
Tehachapi, CA 93561

Tip: The Tehachapi Municipal Airport has offered showers and camping in the past.

CHECK POCKETPCT.COM FOR UPDATES

Tehachapi to Kennedy Meadows

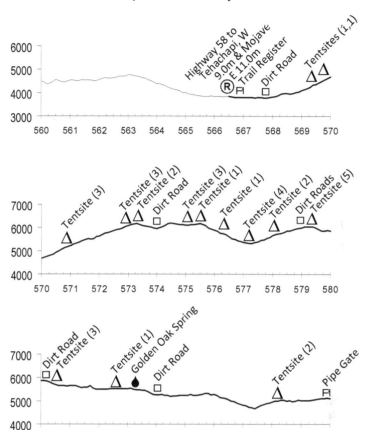

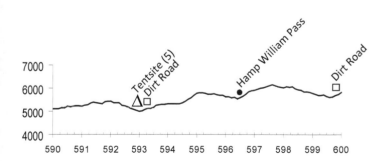

Tehachapi to Kennedy Meadows

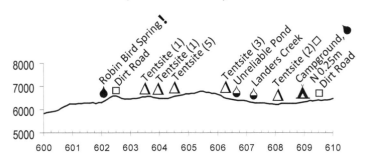

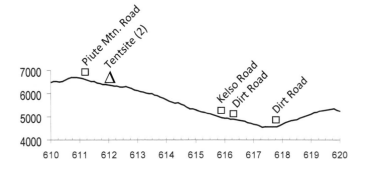

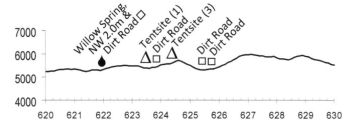

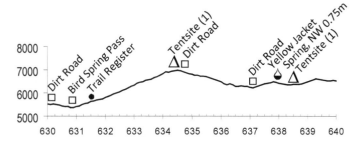

Tehachapi to Kennedy Meadows

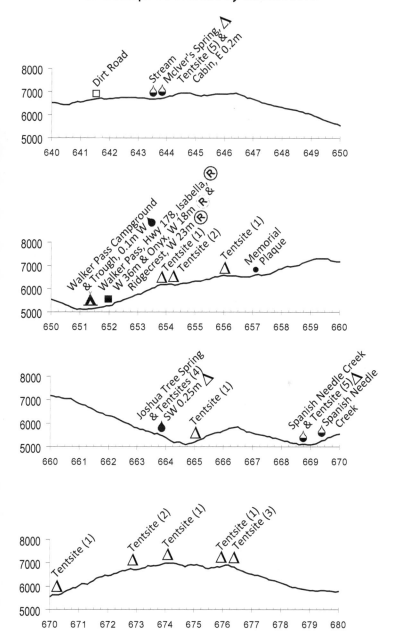

Tehachapi to Kennedy Meadows

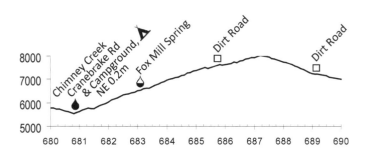

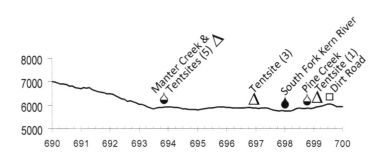

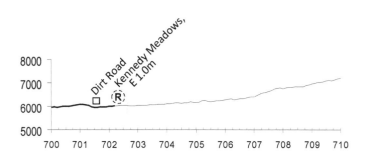

Tehachapi Mile 566 W 9 miles Population: 13,258

U.S. Post Office, 661-822-0279, M-F 9-5, Sa 10-2
Tehachapi, CA 93561

Tip: The Tehachapi Municipal Airport has offered showers and camping in the past.

Tehachapi to Kennedy Meadows

Mojave   Mile 566 E 11 miles   Population: 1,238

U.S. Post Office, 661-824-3502, M-F 9-1, 2-4
Mojave, CA 93501

Tip: Call Kern Regional Transit at 800-323-2396 to schedule bus pickup from the Highway 58 overpass to Mojave or Tehachapi.

Onyx   Mile 652 W 18 miles   Population: 475

U.S. Post Office, 760-378-2121, M-F 9-12, 1-4
Onyx, CA 93255

Tip: A small market is about 0.7 miles SW of the Post Office.

Lake Isabella   Mile 652 W 36 miles   Population: 3,466

P.O., US Mail, 760-379-8755, M-F 10-4
Lake Isabella, CA 93240

Tip: You can catch a bus from Walker Pass to Lake Isabella, Onyx, Inyokern or Ridgecrest. Call 800-323-2396 for details.

Inyokern   Mile 652 E 16.5 miles   Population: 1,099

P.O., US Mail, 800-275-8777, M-F 11-4
Inyokern, CA 93527

Tip: The convenience store is well-stocked and hiker-friendly.

Ridgecrest   Mile 652 E 26.6 miles   Population: 28,600

P.O., US Mail, 760-375-1939, M-F 10-5, Sa 10-2
Ridgecrest, CA 93555

Tip: This town is very spread out, but everything you need is near the post office.

Cost Saving Tip: Make a checklist of all your must-do tasks prior to arriving in town.

CHECK POCKETPCT.COM FOR UPDATES

Kennedy Meadows Mile 702 SE 0.7 miles Population: 200

US Mail or UPS, 559-850-5647, $Fee per box, verify service
c/o Kennedy Meadows
General Store,
96740 Beach Meadows Road
Inyokern, CA 93527

Tip: Send your bear can and any snow equipment you need for t
High Sierra here.

Cost Saving Tip: Avoid mailing multiple packages. Most
businesses charge a fee per box.

Kennedy Meadows to Lake Edison

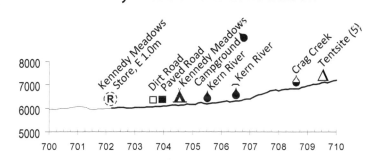

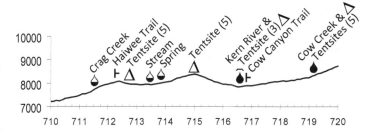

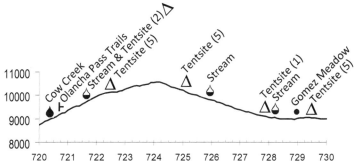

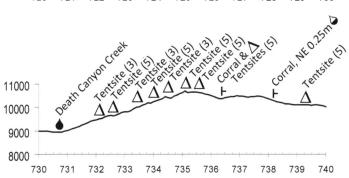

Kennedy Meadows to Lake Edison

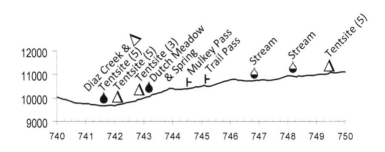

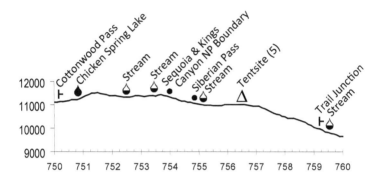

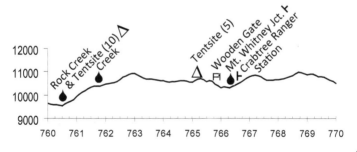

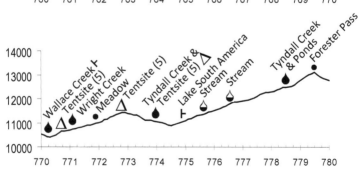

Kennedy Meadows to Lake Edison

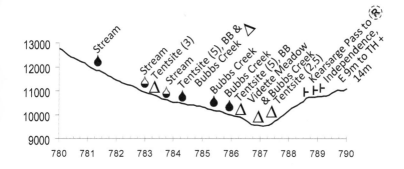

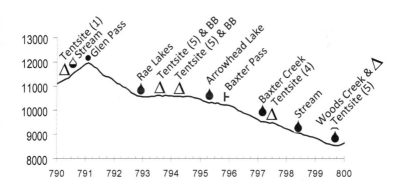

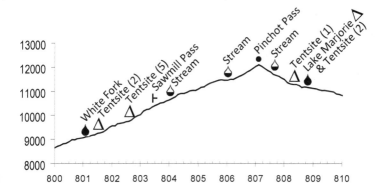

Kennedy Meadows to Lake Edison

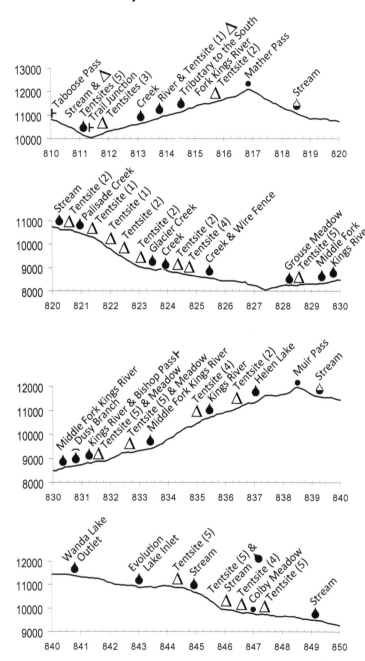

Kennedy Meadows to Lake Edison

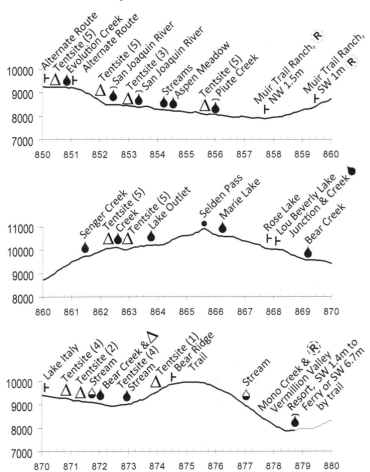

Kennedy Meadows   Mile 702 SE 0.7 miles   Population: 200

US Mail or UPS, 559-850-5647, $Fee per box, verify service
**c/o Kennedy Meadows
General Store,
96740 Beach Meadows Road
Inyokern, CA 93527**

Tip: Send your bear can and any snow equipment you need for the High Sierra here.

CHECK POCKETPCT.COM FOR UPDATES

Kennedy Meadows to Lake Edison

Lone Pine   Mile 745 E 2m + NE 23m   Population: 2,035

U.S. Post Office, 760-876-5681, M-F 9:30-12:30 & 1:30-4:30
Lone Pine, CA 93545

Tip: The Mt. Whitney Hostel is an affordable lodging option in the middle of town (mountwhitneyportal.com).

Independence   Mile 789 E 9m + NE 15m   Population: 669

U.S. Post Office, 760-878-2210, M-F 9:30-12:45 & 1:15-4
Independence, CA 93526

Tip: The Chevron gas station has showers and laundry.

Bishop   Mile 789 E 9m + NE 57m   Population: 3,863

U.S. Post Office, 800-275-8777, M-F 9-4 & Sa 9-1
Bishop, CA 93514

Tip: Check out The Hostel California (thehostelcalifornia.com).

Muir Trail Ranch   Mile 858 NW 1.5 m   Population: 0

Visit muirtrailranch.com for current package mailing details and services. Muir Trail Ranch is a private guest ranch.

Tip: Likely the best hiker box on the PCT. Muir Trail Ranch has limited supplies for sale.

Vermillion Valley Resort   Mile 879 SW 6.7m   Population: 0

Visit edisonlake.com for current package mailing details.

Tip: The first beverage is free.

Cost Saving Tip: Clean and inspect your water filter at every town stop. This will drastically increase the life of your filter.

CHECK POCKETPCT.COM FOR UPDATES

Lake Edison to Tuolumne Meadows

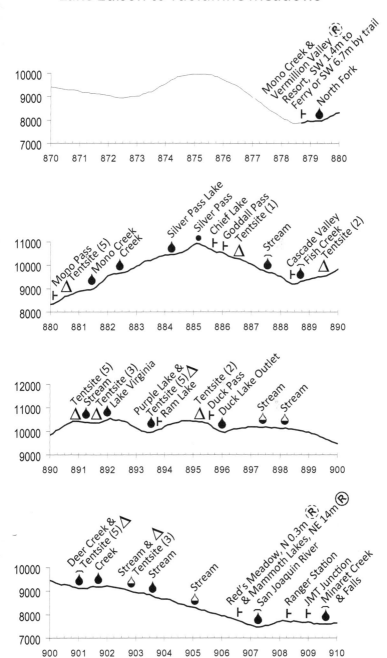

Lake Edison to Tuolumne Meadows

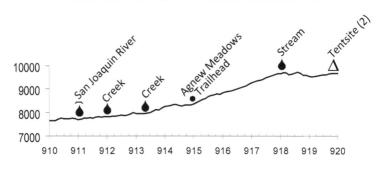

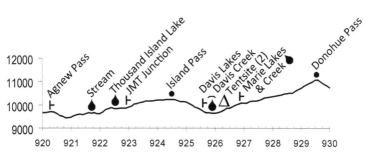

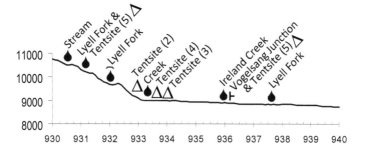

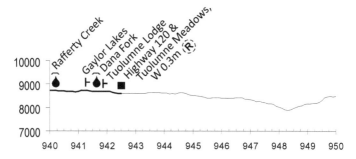

Lake Edison to Tuolumne Meadows

Vermillion Valley Resort Mile 879 SW 6.7m Population: 0

Visit edisonlake.com for current package mailing details.

Tip: The first beverage is free.

Red's Meadow Mile 907 N 0.3m Population: 0

Visit redsmeadow.com for current package mailing details.

Tip: Catch the bus from here to Mammoth Lakes.

Mammoth Lakes Mile 907 NE 14m Population: 8,073

U.S. Post Office, 760-934-2205, M-F 8-4
Mammoth Lakes, CA 93546

Moderne Hostel moderne-hostel.californiahotels24.com
Davison Street Guest House (hostel) mammoth-guest.com

Tip: Davison Street Guest House is very hiker friendly.

Lee Vining Mile 942 E 21m Population: 222

U.S. Post Office, 760-647-6371, M-F 9-1, 2-4
Lee Vining, CA 93541

Tip: Whoa Nellie Deli at the Mobil gas station is famous for its exceptional food. The RV Park has camping, laundry, internet and showers.

Tuolumne Meadows Mile 942 W 0.3m Population: 0

U.S. Post Office, Seasonal, 209-372-8236, M-F 9-5, Sa 9-12
CPU Tuolumne Meadows
Yosemite National Park, CA 95389-9906

Tip: Affordable hiker campsites are available in the campground. Tuolumne Meadows Lodge has showers.

CHECK POCKETPCT.COM FOR UPDATES

Tuolumne Meadows to Echo Lake

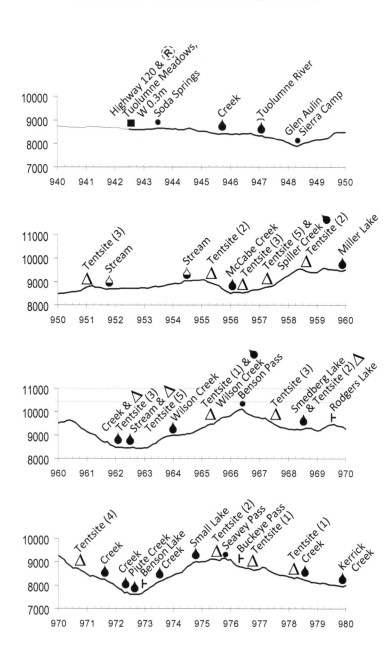

Tuolumne Meadows to Echo Lake

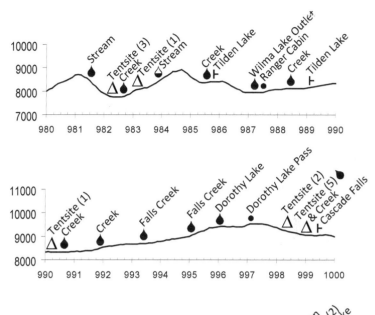

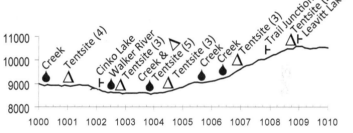

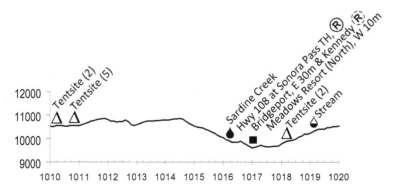

Tuolumne Meadows to Echo Lake

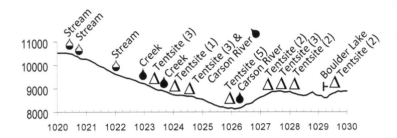

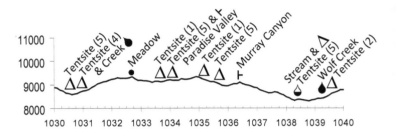

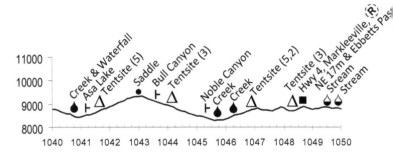

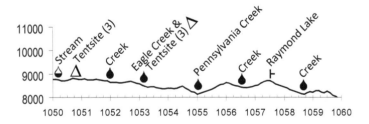

42

Tuolumne Meadows to Echo Lake

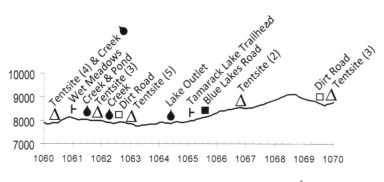

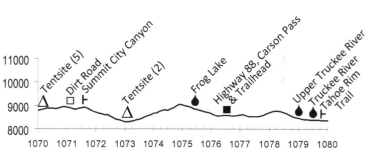

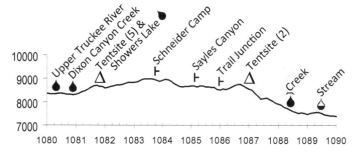

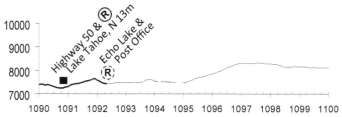

Tuolumne Meadows to Echo Lake

Tuolumne Meadows   Mile 942 W 0.3m   Population: 0

U.S. Post Office, Seasonal, 209-372-8236, M-F 9-5, Sa 9-12
CPU Tuolumne Meadows
Yosemite National Park, CA 95389-9906

Tip: Affordable hiker campsites are available in the campground. Tuolumne Meadows Lodge has showers.

Lee Vining   Mile 942 E 21m   Population: 222

U.S. Post Office, 760-647-6371, M-F 9-1, 2-4
Lee Vining, CA 93541

Tip: Whoa Nellie Deli at the Mobil gas station is famous for its exceptional food. The RV Park has camping, laundry, internet and showers.

Bridgeport   Mile 1017 E 30m   Population: 575

U.S. Post Office, 760-932-7991, M-F 8-12 & 1-4
Bridgeport, CA 93517

Tip: The library has free internet 24 hours a day.

Northern Kennedy Meadows   Mile 1017 W 10m   Pop: 0

Visit kennedymeadows.com for current details
c/o Kennedy Meadows Resort and Pack Station
57 Miles East of Sonora on Hwy 108
Sonora, CA 95370

Tip: Showers and laundry services are available at the resort.

Markleeville   Mile 1048 NE 17m   Population: 210

U.S. Post Office, 530-694-2125, M-F 8:30-11 & 12-3:30 & Sa 8:30-10:30
Markleeville, CA 96120

Tip: The small grocery store is hiker-friendly.

CHECK POCKETPCT.COM FOR UPDATES

Tuolumne Meadows to Echo Lake

South Lake Tahoe   Mile 1091 N 13m   Population: 60

U.S. Post Office is located at 1046 Al Tahoe Blvd.,
530-544-5867, M-F 8:30-5 & Sa 12-2
South Lake Tahoe, CA 96150

Tip: Lake of the Sky Outfitters has a hiker lounge. You can
do your laundry and take a shower at the RV park near
the Apex Hotel.

Echo Lake   Mile 1092 On Trail   Population: 60

Visit echochalet.com for details
U.S. Post Office*, 530-659-7207, M-Sa 11-2
Echo Lake, CA 95721

Tip: Ice cream can be purchased at the Chalet.
*Verify Service- owner may reject hiker packages

Cost Saving Tip: Arriving to town early in the morning
and leaving in the afternoon is a great way to save on
lodging expenses.

Echo Lake to Sierra City

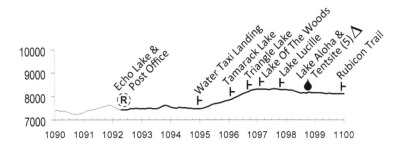

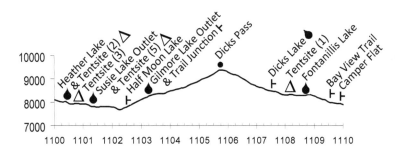

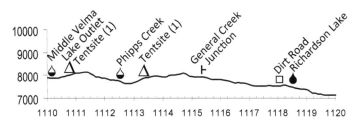

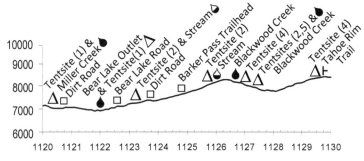

Echo Lake to Sierra City

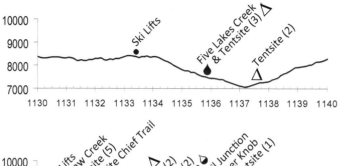

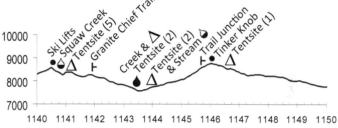

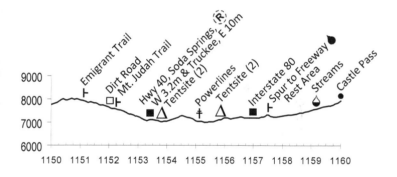

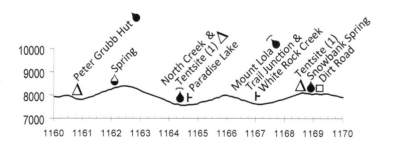

Echo Lake to Sierra City

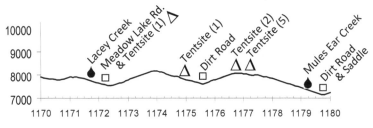

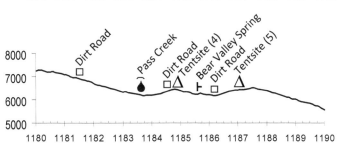

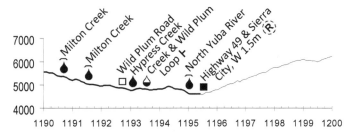

Echo Lake   Mile 1092 On Trail   Population: 60

Visit echochalet.com for details
U.S. Post Office*, 530-659-7207, M-Sa 11-2
Echo Lake, CA 95721

Tip: Ice cream can be purchased at the Chalet.
*Verify Service- owner may reject hiker packages

Truckee   Mile 1153 E 10m   Population: 16,165

U.S. Post Office, 530-587-7158, M-F 8:30-5 & Sa 11-2
Truckee, CA 96161

Tip: The Visitor Center is extremely helpful and has wifi.

CHECK POCKETPCT.COM FOR UPDATES

Echo Lake to Sierra City

Soda Springs
Mile 1153 W 3.2 m   Population: 0

U.S. Post Office, 530-426-3082, M-F 9-1, 1:30-3:30
Soda Springs, CA 95728

The Clair Tappaan Lodge Lodge (1.4 miles West of the PCT) offers hostel-like accommodation, showers and laundry.

Tip: Donner Ski Ranch Restaurant and Bar is West 0.2 miles from the Highway 40 crossing. It is worth the side trip.

Sierra City
Mile 1195 W 1.5m   Population: 221

U.S. Post Office, 530-862-1152, M-F 10-2, Sa 10:30-12:30
Sierra City, CA 96125

Visit sierracountrystore.com for package mailing instructions.

Tip: The General Store has amazing hamburgers.

Cost Saving Tip: The Methodist Church in Sierra City may provide free camping.

Sierra City to Belden

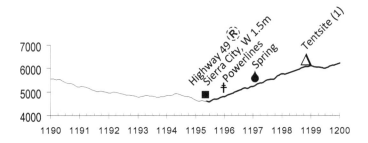

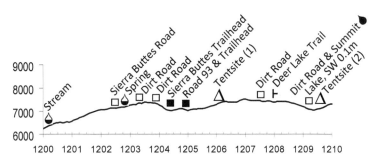

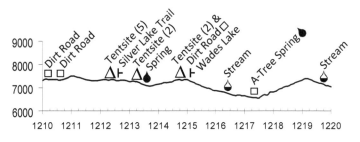

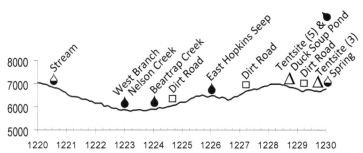

Sierra City to Belden

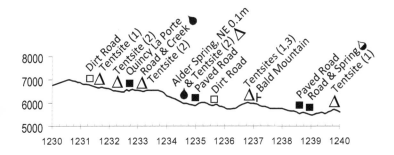

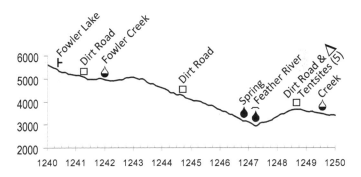

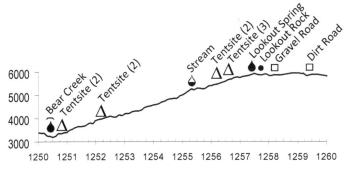

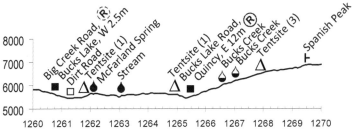

Sierra City to Belden

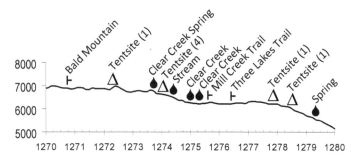

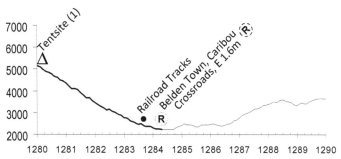

Sierra City   Mile 1153 W 1.5m   Population: 221

U.S. Post Office, 530-862-1152, M-F 10-2, Sa 10:30-12:30
Sierra City, CA 96125

Visit sierracountrystore.com for package mailing instructions.

Tip: The General Store has amazing hamburgers.

Bucks Lake   Mile 1261 SW 2.5m   Population: 10

Visit buckslakelodge.com or call 530-283-2262 for package maili
details.

Tip: Bucks Lake Lodge (not to be confused with Bucks Lake Mari
is extremely hiker-friendly. Free beer or ice cream has been offe
to hikers in the past.   Ask for Lou.

CHECK POCKETPCT.COM FOR UPDATES

Sierra City to Belden

Quincy Mile 1265 E 12m Population: 1,728

U.S. Post Office, 530-283-3912, M-F 8:30-5
Quincy, CA 95971

Tip: Gold Pan Lodge is hiker-friendly. There is a health food store in town.

Belden Mile 1284 On Trail Population: 22

Tip: A local trail angel may provide a place to stay and package services. Check pocketpct.com for details.

Caribou Crossroads Mile 1284 E 1.9m Population: 0

Visit cariboucrossroads.com for additional details.
U.S. Post Office, Limited Postal Services, 530-283-1384, M-Sa 7-6
c/o Caribou Crossroads
16242 Highway 70
Belden, CA 95915-1415

Tip: Milkshakes are pretty good here.

Cost Saving Tip: Consider sharing the washer when doing laundry. Pre-rinse dirty socks before washing.

Belden to Old Station

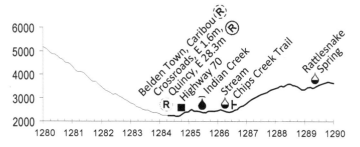

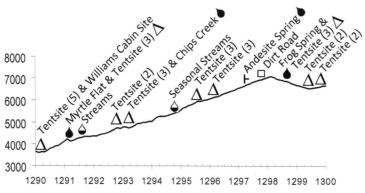

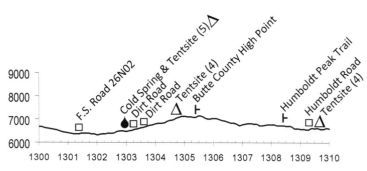

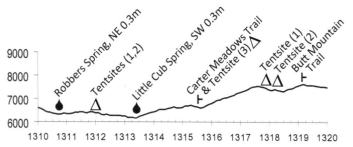

Belden to Old Station

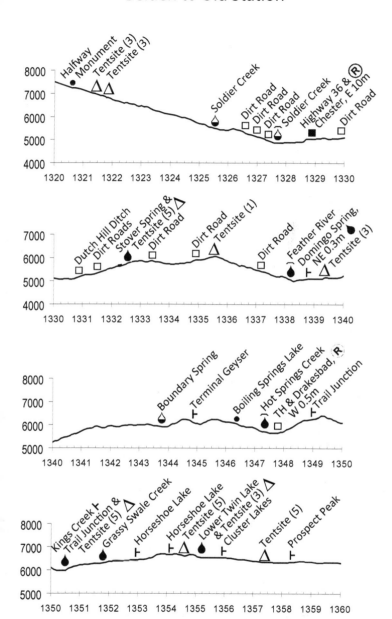

Belden to Old Station

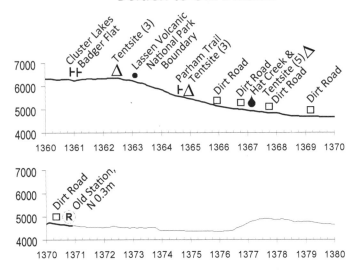

Belden Mile 1284 On Trail Population: 22

> Tip: Local trail angel may provide a place to stay and accept packages. Check pocketpct.com for details.

Caribou Crossroads Mile 1284 E 1.9m Population: 0

> Visit cariboucrossroads.com for additional details.
> U.S. Post Office, Limited Postal Services, 530-283-1384, M-Sa 7-6
> **c/o Caribou Crossroads**
> **16242 Highway 70**
> **Belden, CA 95915-1415**

> Tip: Milkshakes are pretty good here.

Chester Mile 1329 E 10m Population: 2144

> U.S. Post Office, M-F 8:30-4, 530-258-4184
> **Chester, CA 96020**

> Tip: The Pine Shack has JUMBO milkshakes.

CHECK POCKETPCT.COM FOR UPDATES

Drakesbad Mile 1348 W 0.5m Population: 0

UPS, Fed Ex or US Mail, 866-999-0914,
Visit drakesbad.com for additional details
c/o Drakesbad Guest Ranch
End of Warner Valley Road
Chester, CA 96020

Tip: Check out the hot spring pool.

Cost Saving Tip: There are a few campsites just
north of Warner Valley Campground near Drakesbad.
Camping here will save you from paying at the
campground.

Old Station Mile 1371 N 0.3m Population: 51

U.S. Post Office, 530-335-7191, M-F 11-3
Old Station, CA 96071

Tip: The nearby "resort" has showers, laundry and
tentsites.

Cost Saving Tip: Inspect and clean your tent zipper at
every town stop. This will increase the life of your tent
zipper.

Old Station to Burney Falls

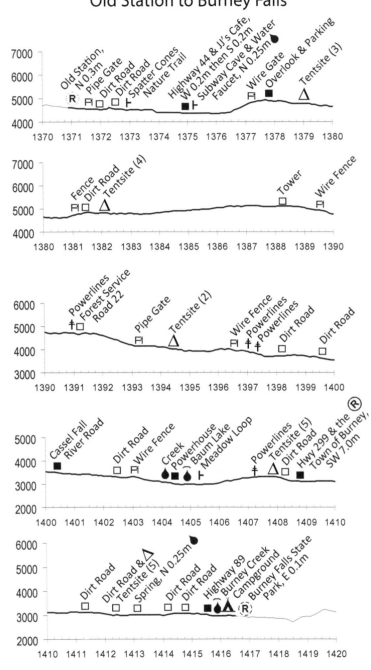

Old Station to Burney Falls

Old Station   Mile 1371 N 0.3m Population: 51

U.S. Post Office, 530-335-7191, M-F 11-3
Old Station, CA 96071

Tip: The nearby "resort" has showers, laundry and tentsites.

JJ's Cafe & Resort   Mile 1375 W 0.2m & S 0.4m   Population: 0

Visit jjscafeoldstation.com for hours. Rim Rock Ranch Resort is located SW 0.2 miles of JJ's Cafe. Visit rimrockcabins.com for additional details.

Tip: When you cross Highway 44 at mile 1375 turn left (West) then turn left (South) on Highway 89. The 0.6 mile side trip to JJ's Cafe is worth it.

Burney   Mile 1409 SW 7m   Population: 3,154

U.S. Post Office, 530-335-5430, M-F 9:30-4
Burney, CA 96013

Tip: Getting a ride to Burney can be difficult.

Burney Falls State Park   Mile 1416 E 0.1m   Population: 0

UPS Only, 530-335-5713, Open Daily, $Fee per box
c/o Burney Falls Camp Store
McArthur Burney Falls State Park
24900 State Highway 89
Burney, CA 96013

Tip: The General Store has wifi. Coin operated showers are located in the Burney Falls State Park.

Cost Saving Tip: Save money by mailing a package to the Burney Falls Camp Store. Burney Falls Camp Store has limited supplies.

CHECK POCKETPCT.COM FOR UPDATES

Burney Falls to Castella

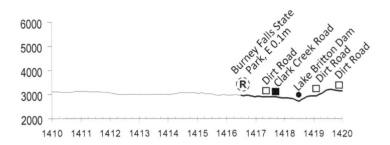

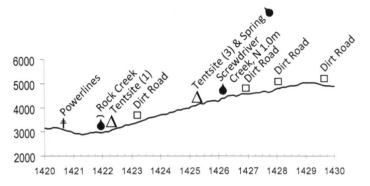

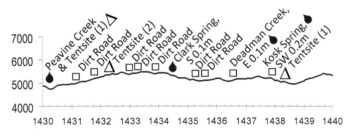

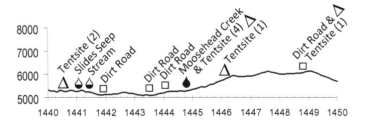

Burney Falls to Castella

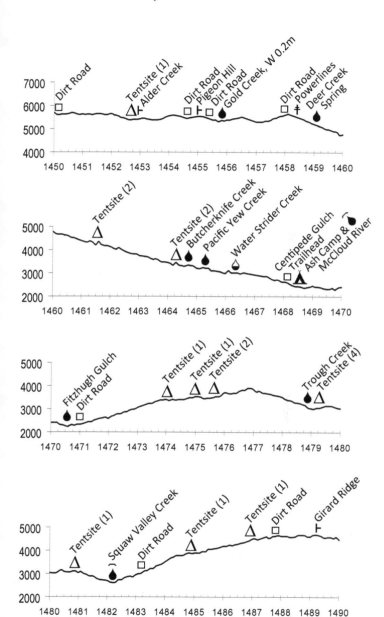

Burney Falls to Castella

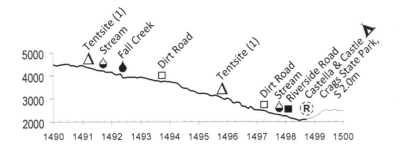

Burney Falls State Park   Mile 1416 E 0.1m   Population: 0

UPS Only, 530-335-5713, Open Daily, $Fee per box
c/o Burney Falls Camp Store
McArthur Burney Falls State Park
24900 State Highway 89
Burney, CA 96013

Tip: The General Store has wifi.

Mount Shasta   Mile 1499 N 15m   Population: 3,292

U.S. Post Office, 530-926-1343, M-F 8:30-5
Shasta, CA 96067

Tip: Fifth Season outfitters is very hiker-friendly and has a great selection of gear for hikers.

Dunsmuir   Mile 1499 N 4.5m   Population: 1,583

U.S. Post Office, 530-235-0338, M-F 8:30-5
Dunsmuir, CA 96025

Tip: Dunsmuir has an Amtrak stop.

Burney Falls to Castella

Castella   Mile 1499 S 2.0m   Population: 240

U.S. Post Office, 530-235-4413, M-F 11-3, Sa 8:45-10
Castella, CA 96017

Ammirati's Market is Open Daily 8-9, 530-235-2676

US Mail
c/o Ammirati's Market
P.O. Box 90
Castella, CA 96017

UPS or FedEx
c/o Ammirati's Market
20107 Castle Creek Road
Castella, CA 96017

Tip: Castle Crags State Park has a hiker area and showers. It is fairly easy to get a ride to the town of Mount Shasta from the Castella area.

Cost Saving Tip: There is a hiker camping rate at the Castle Crags State Park.

Castella to Seiad Valley

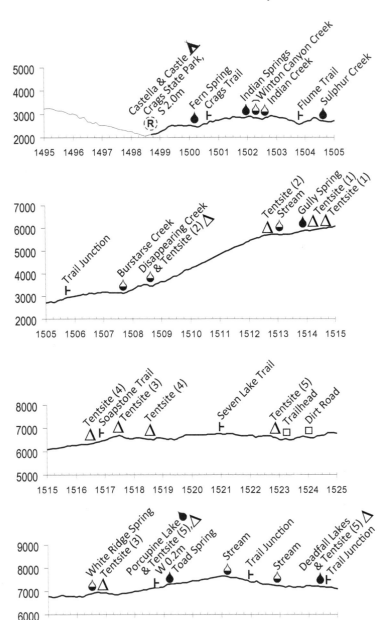

Castella to Seiad Valley

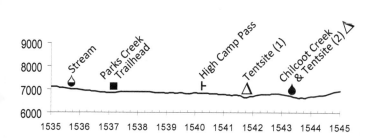

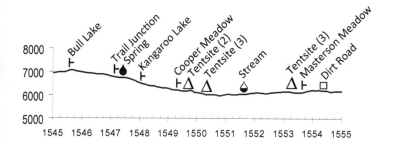

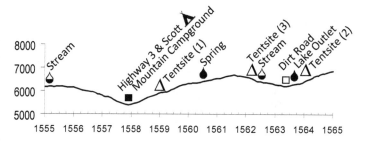

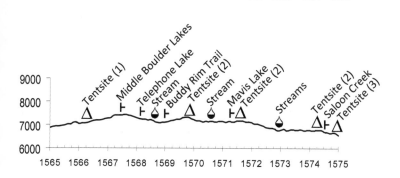

Castella to Seiad Valley

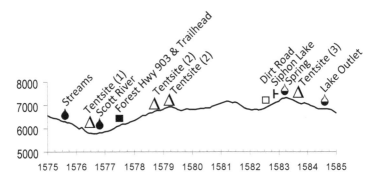

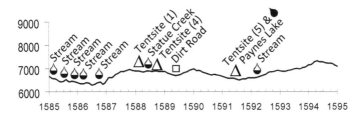

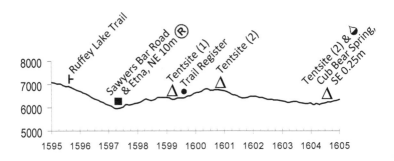

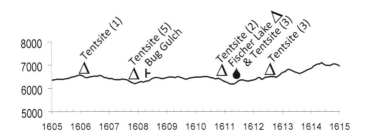

Castella to Seiad Valley

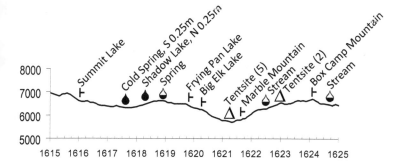

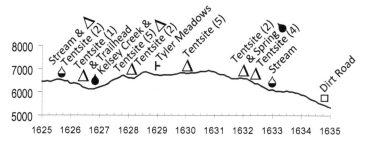

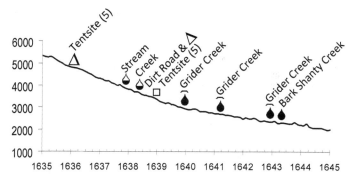

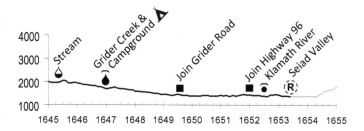

Castella to Seiad Valley

Castella Mile 1499 S 2.0m Population: 240

U.S. Post Office, 530-235-4413, M-F 11-3 & 1-4:30, Sa 8:45-10
Castella, CA 96017

Ammirati's Market is Open Daily 8-9, 530-235-2676
US Mail   UPS or FedEx
c/o Ammirati's Market   c/o Ammirati's Market
P.O. Box 90   20107 Castle Creek Road
Castella, CA 96017   Castella, CA 96017

Tip: Castle Crags State Park has a hiker area and showers. It is fairly easy to get a ride to the town of Mount Shasta from the Castella area.

Etna Mile 1597 NE 10m Population: 719

U.S. Post Office, 530-467-3981, M-F 9-5
Etna, CA 96027

Hikers Hut
Visit alderbrookmanor.com for package mailing details.

Tip: Check out the Etna Brewery and the RV park.

Seiad Valley Mile 1653 On Trail Population: 300

U.S Post Office, 530-496-3211, M-F 12-4, Sa 12-1:30
Seiad Valley, CA 96086

UPS or US Mail, 530-496-3399, Open Daily 6-9 Verify Service
c/o Seiad Valley Store
44719 Highway 96
Seiad Valley CA 96086

Tip: Home of the famous pancake challenge.

Cost Saving Tip: The Mid River RV Park in Seiad Valley has a backpacker rate, laundry and showers.

Seiad Valley to Ashland

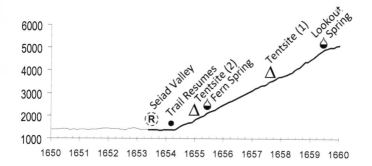

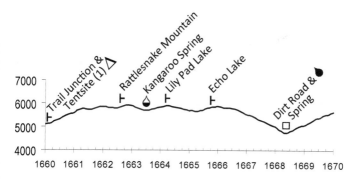

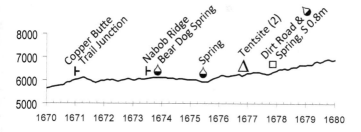

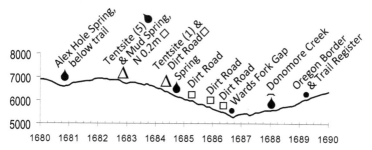

Seiad Valley to Ashland

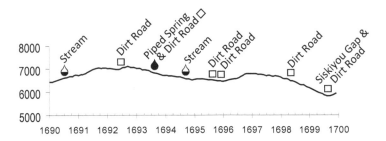

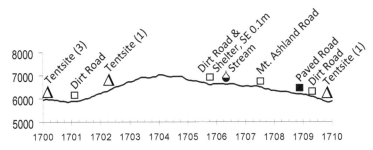

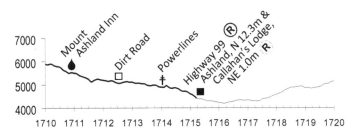

Seiad Valley   Mile 1653 On Trail   Population: 300

U.S Post Office, 530-496-3211, M-F 12-4, Sa 12-1:30
Seiad Valley, CA 96086

UPS or US Mail, 530-496-3399, Open Daily 6-9 Verify Service
c/o Seiad Valley Store
44719 Highway 96
Seiad Valley CA 96086

Tip: Home of the famous pancake challenge.

CHECK POCKETPCT.COM FOR UPDATES

Seiad Valley to Ashland

Callahan's Lodge   Mile 1715 NE 1.0m Population: 0

US Mail or UPS, 541-482-1299, Open Daily, $Fee per box
Visit callahanslodge.com for current details
c/o Callahan's Lodge
7100 Old Highway 99 South
Ashland, OR 97520

Tip: Callahan's offers a great hiker special. This is a good
place to find a ride into Ashland.

Ashland   Mile 1715 N 12.3m Population: 20,713

U.S. Post Office, 541-552-1622, M-F 9-5
Ashland, OR 97520

Tip: There are a couple of hostels in town
(theashlandhostel.com 541-482-9217 and
ashlandcommons.com 541-482-6753). Ashland is the
home of a famous Shakespeare festival.

Cost Saving Tip: If heading into Ashland consider buying
and mailing food all the way up to Timberline Lodge. You
can then buy and mail food in Cascade Locks for the entire
state of Washington.

Ashland to Crater Lake

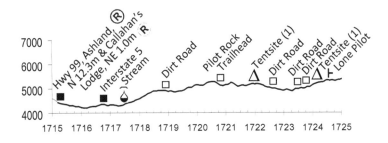

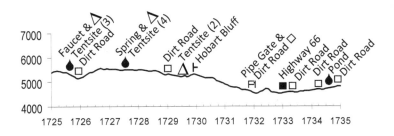

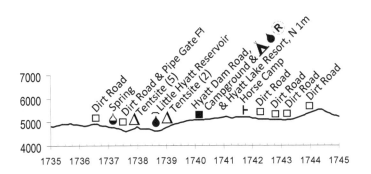

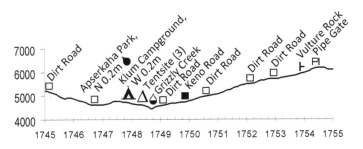

Ashland to Crater Lake

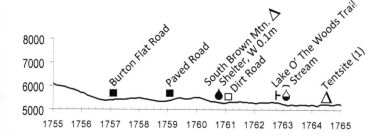

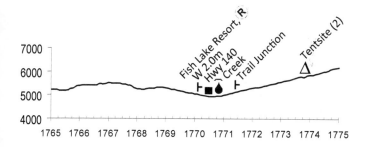

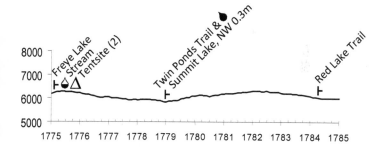

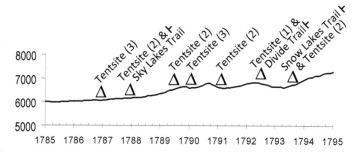

Ashland to Crater Lake

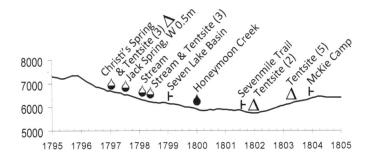

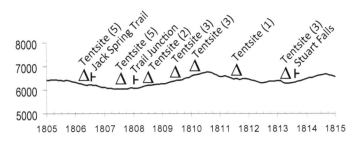

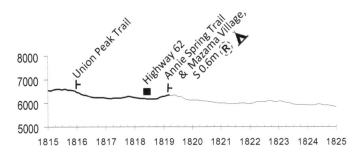

Ashland   Mile 1715 N 12.3m Population: 20,713

U.S. Post Office, 541-552-1622, M-F 9-5
Ashland, OR 97520

Tip: There are a couple of hostels in town
(theashlandhostel.com 541-482-9217 and
ashlandcommons.com 541-482-6753). Ashland is the
home of a famous Shakespeare festival.

CHECK POCKETPCT.COM FOR UPDATES

Ashland to Crater Lake

Callahan's Lodge Mile 1715 NE 1.0m Population: 0

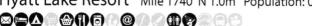

US Mail or UPS, 541-482-1299, Open Daily, $Fee per box
Visit callahanslodge.com for current details
c/o Callahan's Lodge
7100 Old Highway 99 South
Ashland, OR 97520

Tip: Callahan's offers a great hiker special. This is a good place to find a ride into Ashland.

Hyatt Lake Resort Mile 1740 N 1.0m Population: 0

UPS Only, 541-482-3331, Open Daily, 8-5, hyattlake.com
c/o Hyatt Lake Resort
7900 Hyatt Prairie Road
Ashland, OR 97520

Tip: The campground has showers.

Fish Lake Resort Mile 1770 W 2.0m Population: 0

UPS Only, 541-949-8500, Visit fishlakeresort.net for details
c/o Fish Lake Resort
State Hwy 140, Mile Marker 30
Medford, OR 97501

Tip: Laundry and showers are located in the campground.

Crater Lake NP Mile 1819 S 0.6m Population: 0

541-594-2255, Open Daily, Hours Vary

US Mail	UPS Only
c/o Mazama Village Store	**c/o Mazama Village Store**
P.O. Box 158	**569 Mazama Village Drive**
Crater Lake, OR 97604	**Crater Lake, OR 97604**

Tip: Showers and laundry are located near the Village Store.

Cost Saving Tip: Mazama Village Campground allows six people per campsite (about $4 per person).

CHECK POCKETPCT.COM FOR UPDATES

Crater Lake to Shelter Cove

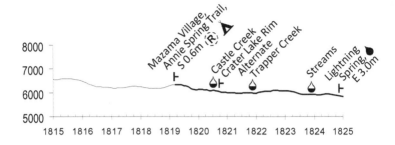

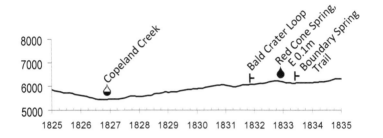

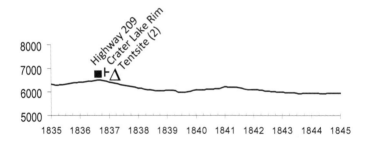

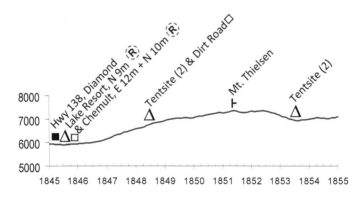

Crater Lake to Shelter Cove

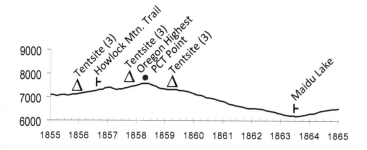

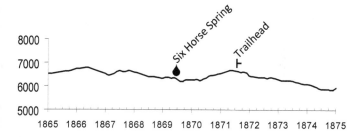

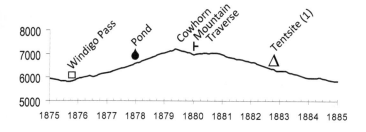

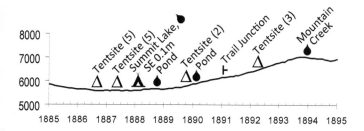

Crater Lake to Shelter Cove

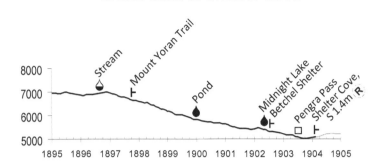

Crater Lake NP Mile 1819 S 0.6m Population: 0

541-594-2255, Open Daily, Hours Vary

US Mail
c/o Mazama Village Store
P.O. Box 158
Crater Lake, OR 97604

UPS Only
c/o Mazama Village Store
569 Mazama Village Drive
Crater Lake, OR 97604

Tip: Showers and laundry are located near the Village Store.

Diamond Lake Mile 1845 W 1.2m + N 8m Population: 0

UPS Only, 541-793-3333, Open Daily
Visit diamondlake.net for current details
c/o Diamond Lake Resort
350 Resort Drive
Diamond Lake, OR 97731

Tip: Diamond Lake Resort has reasonable restaurant prices.

Chemult Mile 1845 E 12m + N 10m Population: 300

U.S. Post Office 541-365-4411, M-F 9-12 & 12:30-3:30
Chemult, OR 97731

Tip: Amtrak train station is located east of town.

Shelter Cove Resort Mile 1904 S 1.4m Population: 0

UPS Only, 541-433-2548, Open Daily
Verify Service, sheltercoveresort.com
c/o Shelter Cove Resort
27600 West Odell Lake Road, Highway 58
Crescent, OR 97733

Tip: The resort has showers and laundry.

Cost Saving Tip: Reduce the number of mailed packages by hiking more miles between town stops. You will save a lot of money on postage and you will avoid costly town expenses.

Shelter Cove to Elk Lake

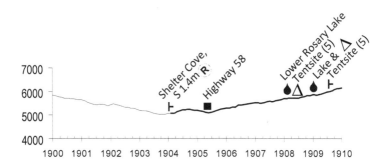

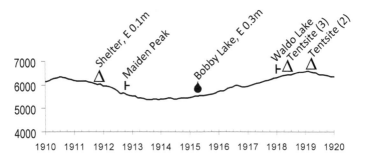

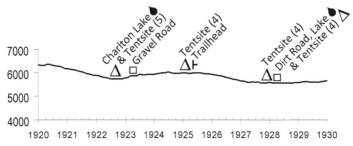

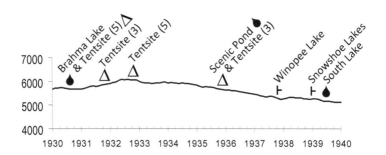

Shelter Cove to Elk Lake

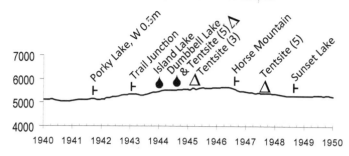

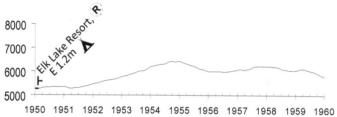

Shelter Cove Resort   Mile 1904 S 1.4m   Population: 0

UPS Only, 541-433-2548, Open Daily
Verify Service, sheltercoveresort.com
c/o Shelter Cove Resort
27600 West Odell Lake Road, Highway 58
Crescent, OR 97733

Tip: The resort has showers and laundry.

Elk Lake Resort   Mile 1950 E 1.2m   Population: 0

UPS or Fed Ex Only, 541-480-7378, Open Daily, $Fee per box
Visit elklakeresort.net for additional details
c/o Elk Lake Resort
60000 SW Century Drive
Bend, OR 97701

Tip: Hiker packages are left out in the open and accessible
to people and animals. Be careful what you send here.

Cost Saving Tip: Consider splitting a campsite with other
hikers when staying in a campground.

CHECK POCKETPCT.COM FOR UPDATES

Elk Lake to Timberline Lodge

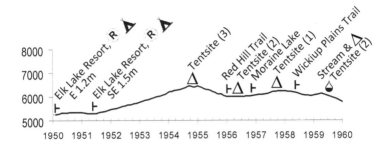

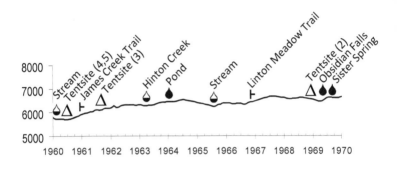

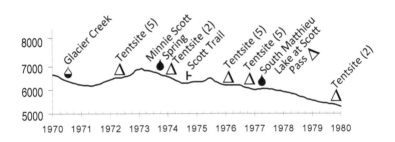

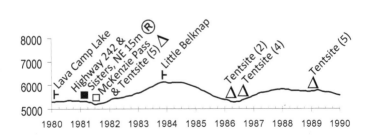

Elk Lake to Timberline Lodge

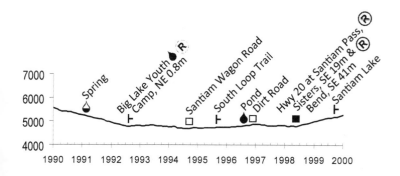

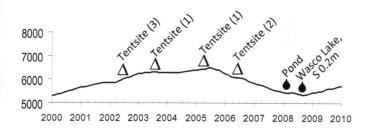

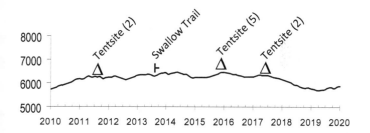

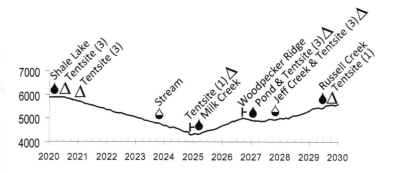

Elk Lake to Timberline Lodge

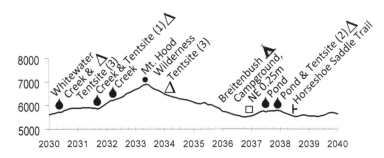

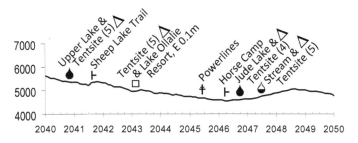

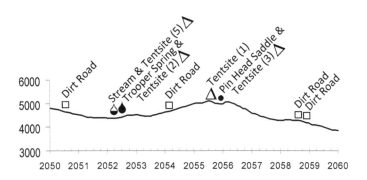

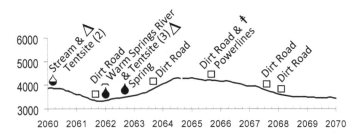

Elk Lake to Timberline Lodge

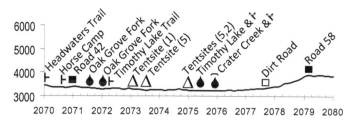

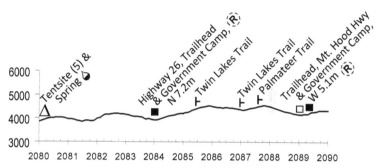

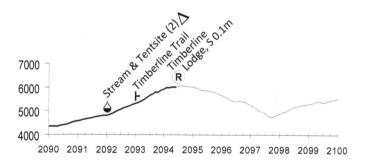

Elk Lake Resort Mile 1950 E 1.2m Population: 0

UPS or Fed Ex Only, 541-480-7378, Open Daily, $Fee per box
Visit elklakeresort.net for additional details
c/o Elk Lake Resort
60000 SW Century Drive
Bend, OR 97701

Tip: Hiker packages are left out in the open and accessible to
people and animals. Be careful what you send here.

CHECK POCKETPCT.COM FOR UPDATES

Elk Lake to Timberline Lodge

Sisters   Mile 1981 E 15m   Population: 2,174
Mile 1998 SE 19m

U.S. Post Office, 541-549-0412, M-F 8:30-5
Sisters, OR 97759

Tip: Sno Cap has delicious specialty shakes.

Bend   Mile 1998 SE 41m   Population: 81,236

U.S. Post Office, 541-318-5068, M-F 8:30-5:30 & Sa 10-1
Bend, OR 97701

Tip: There is a huge REI at 380 SW Powerhouse Drive.

Government Camp   Mile 2084 N 7.2m   Population: 193
Mile 2089 W 5.1m

U.S Post Office, 503-272-3238, M-F 12-4
Government Camp, OR 97028

Tip: There is a Chevron with a Food Mart North 2 miles from
the Highway 26 and PCT crossing (mile 2084).

Timberline Lodge   Mile 2094 S 0.1m   Population: 0

US Mail or UPS, 503-272-3311, Open Daily, $Fee per box
Visit timberlinelodge.com for current details
c/o Wy' East Store
Timberline Lodge Ski Area
27500 E Timberline Rd.
Timberline Lodge, OR 97028

Tip: The lodge is a beautiful U.S. Historic Site and has an
amazing buffet.

Cost Saving Tip: There are some potential campsites just
above Timberline Lodge along the PCT.

CHECK POCKETPCT.COM FOR UPDATES

Timberline Lodge to Cascade Locks

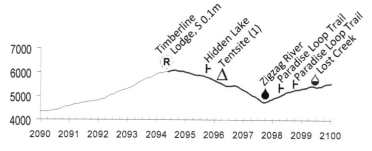

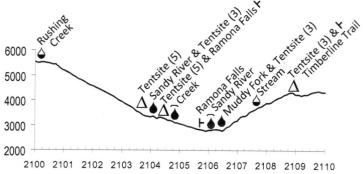

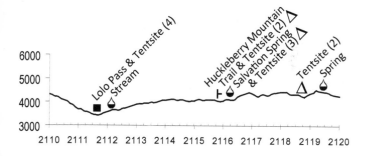

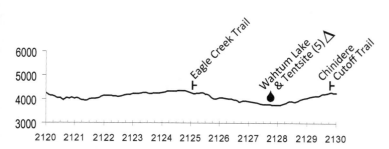

Timberline Lodge to Cascade Locks

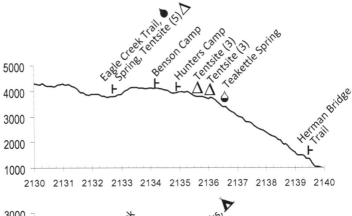

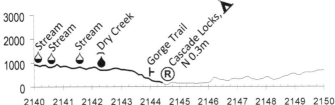

Timberline Lodge   Mile 2094 S 0.1m Population: 0

US Mail or UPS, 503-272-3311, Open Daily, $Fee per box
Visit timberlinelodge.com for current details
c/o Wy' East Store
Timberline Lodge Ski Area
27500 E Timberline Rd.
Timberline Lodge, OR 97028

Tip: The lodge is a beautiful U.S. Historic Site and has an amazing buffet.

Cascade Locks   Mile 2144 N 0.3m Population:1,148

U.S. Post Office, 541-374-5026, M-F 8:30-1 & 2-5
Cascade Locks, OR 97014

Tip: Local Trail Angel Shrek has a house with a shower, laundry, and tenting for PCT hikers.

Cost Saving Tip: Grocery shop in Cascade Locks for the entire state of Washington. Mail packages from the P.O.

CHECK POCKETPCT.COM FOR UPDATES

Cascade Locks to White Pass

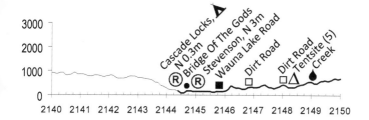

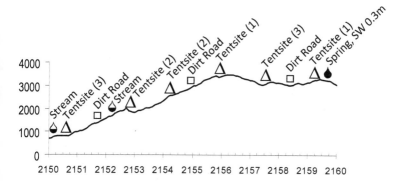

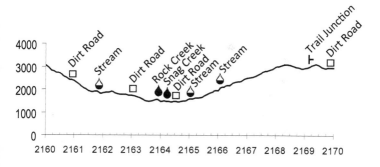

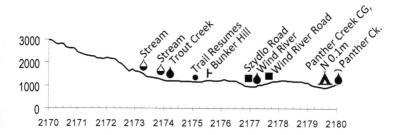

Cascade Locks to White Pass

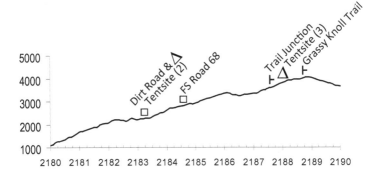

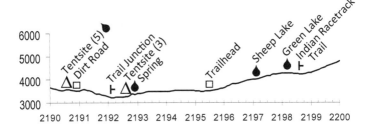

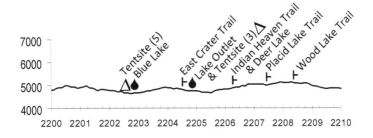

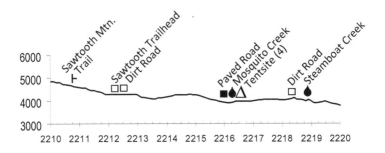

Cascade Locks to White Pass

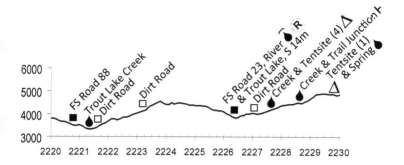

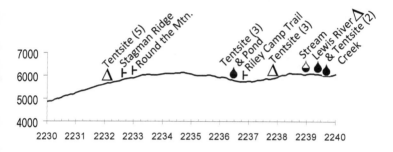

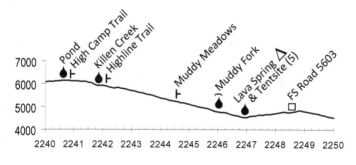

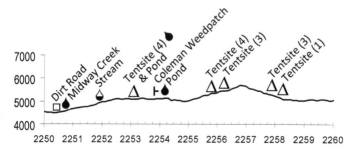

Cascade Locks to White Pass

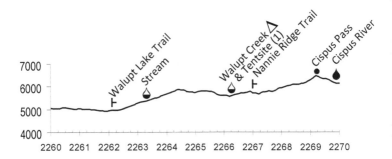

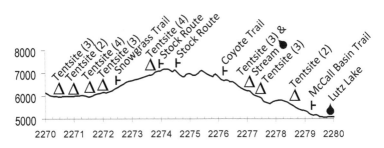

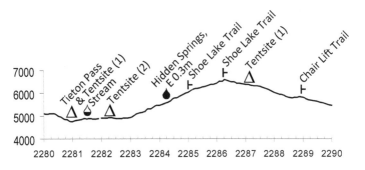

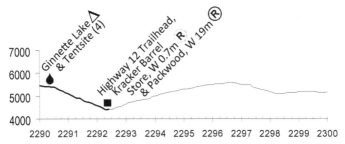

92

Cascade Locks to White Pass

Cascade Locks Mile 2144 N 0.3m Population:1,148

U.S. Post Office, 541-374-5026, M-F 8:30-1 & 2-5
Cascade Locks, OR 97014

Tip: Local Trail Angel Shrek has a house with a shower, laundry, and tenting for PCT hikers.

Stevenson Mile 2145 N 3m Population: 1,494

U.S. Post Office, 541-374-5026, M-F 8:30-5
Stevenson, WA 98648

Tip: Rodeway Inn on the East side of town is one of the only affordable lodging options.

Trout Lake Mile 2226 S 14m Population: 509

U.S. Post Office, 509-395-2108 M-F 9:30-12:30 & 1-4
Trout Lake, WA 98650

Visit troutlakewashington.com for current details
c/o Trout Lake Grocery
2383 Hwy 141
Trout Lake, WA 98650

Tip: Packages are delivered to the general store.

Packwood Mile 2292 W 19m Population: 1,330

U.S. Post Office, 360-494-6311, M-F 8-12 & 1-4:45
Packwood, WA 98361

Tip: Hotel Packwood is very hiker-friendly and affordable.

White Pass Mile 2292 W 0.7m Population: 0

US Mail, 509-672-3105, Open Daily
Kracker Barrel Store
48851 US Highway 12
Naches, WA 98937

Tip: The Kracker Barrel Store has a deli.

CHECK POCKETPCT.COM FOR UPDATES

White Pass to Snoqualmie Pass

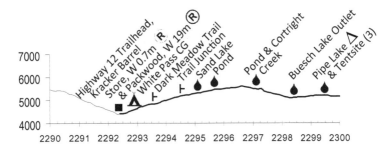

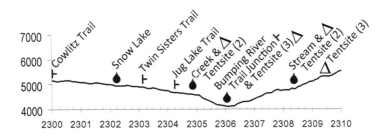

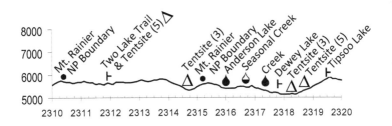

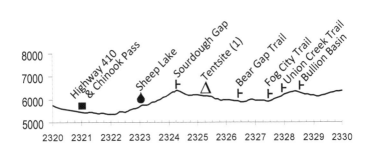

White Pass to Snoqualmie Pass

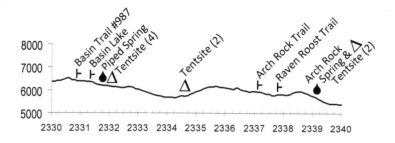

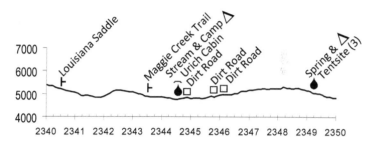

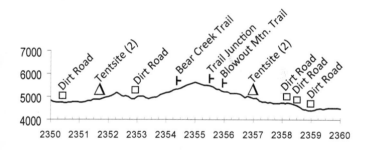

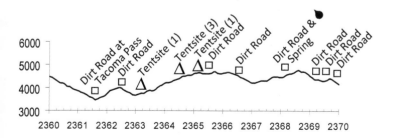

White Pass to Snoqualmie Pass

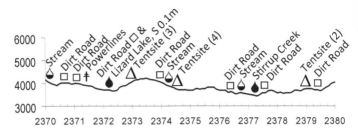

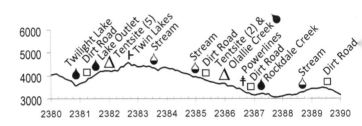

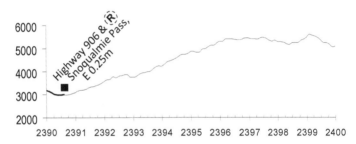

White Pass   Mile 2292 W 0.7m   Population: 0

US Mail, 509-672-3105, Open Daily
Kracker Barrel Store
48851 US Highway 12
Naches, WA 98937

Tip: The Kracker Barrel Store has a deli.

White Pass to Snoqualmie Pass

Packwood   Mile 2292 W 19m   Population: 1,330

U.S. Post Office, 360-494-6311, M-F 8-12 & 1-4:45
Packwood, WA 98361

Tip: Hotel Packwood is very hiker-friendly and affordable.
The RV Park has tentsites, laundry, showers and internet.

Snoqualmie Pass   Mile 2390 E 0.25m   Population: 311

US Mail, ETA Required on package, Verify Service
c/o General Delivery
Snoqualmie Pass, WA 98068
Please Hold at the Chevron
Station for PCT Hiker

U.S. Mail Only, $Fee for non-guests. Open Daily with
extended hours, 425-434-6300, visit
www.snoqualmiesummitinn.com for current details
c/o Summit Inn
P.O. Box 163
Snoqualmie Pass, WA 98068

Tip: The Summit Inn has a hot tub. The DRU
BRU brewery across the street is also worthy of a visit.

Cost Saving Tip: The Aardvark Express next to the Chevron
is an affordable and hiker-friendly place to eat.

Snoqualmie Pass to Skykomish

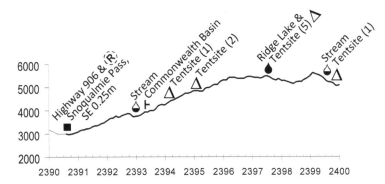

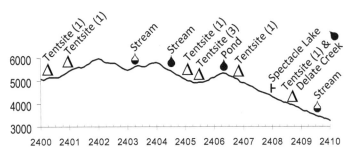

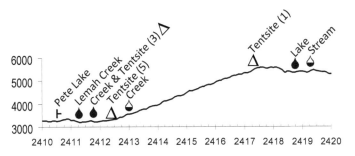

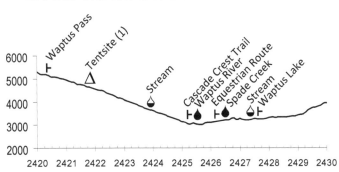

Snoqualmie to Skykomish

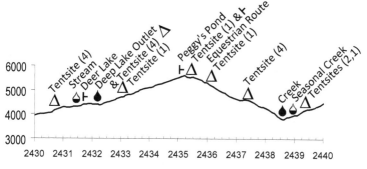

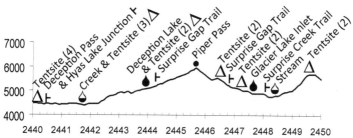

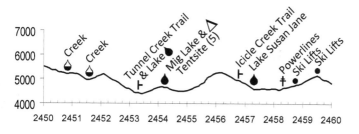

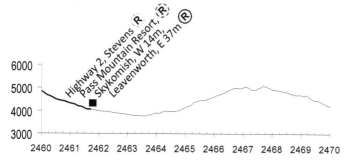

Snoqualmie Pass to Skykomish

Snoqualmie Pass   Mile 2390 E 0.25m Population: 311

US Mail, ETA Required on package, Verify Service
c/o General Delivery
Snoqualmie Pass, WA 98068
Please Hold at the Chevron
Station for PCT Hiker

U.S. Mail Only, $Fee for non-guests. Open Daily with
extended hours, 425-434-6300, visit
www.snoqualmiesummitinn.com for current details
c/o Summit Inn
P.O. Box 163
Snoqualmie Pass, WA 98068

Tip: The Summit Inn has a hot tub. The DRU
BRU brewery across the street is also worthy of a visit.

Stevens Pass Resort   Mile 2462 On Trail Population: 0

UPS or FED EX Only, 206-812-7844, check stevenspass.com
for business hours and current details.
c/o Stevens Pass, Through Hiker
93001 NE Stevens Pass Hwy, US 2
Skykomish, WA 98288

Leavenworth   Mile 2462 E 37m Population: 1,992

U.S. Post Office, US Mail, 509-548-7212, M-F 9-5 & Sa 9-11
Leavenworth, WA 98826

Tip: Leavenworth is styled as a Bavarian Village and is
overrun with tourists.

Skykomish   Mile 2462 W 14m Population: 205

U.S. Post Office, 360-677-2241, M-F 8-11:30 & 12-3:45 & Sa 8-10
Skykomish, WA 98288

Check out the Dinsmores at www.dinsmoreshikerhaven.com

Tip: Cascadia Inn offers affordable lodging and has a nice cafe.

CHECK POCKETPCT.COM FOR UPDATES

Skykomish to Stehekin

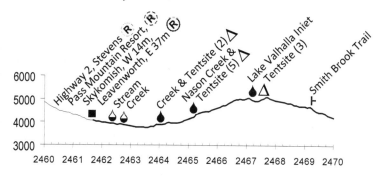

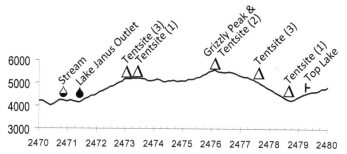

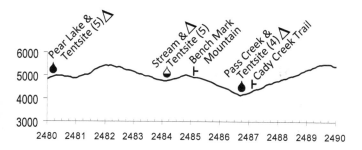

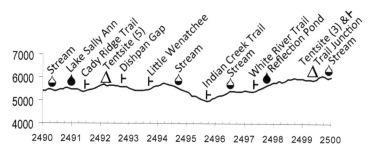

Skykomish to Stehekin

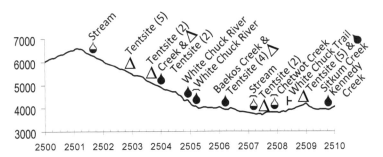

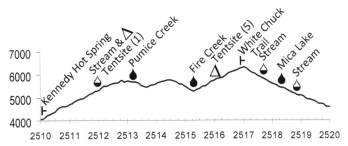

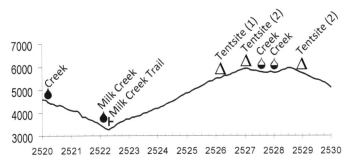

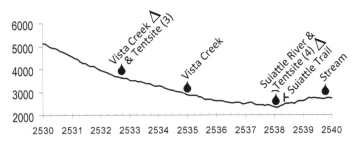

102

Skykomish to Stehekin

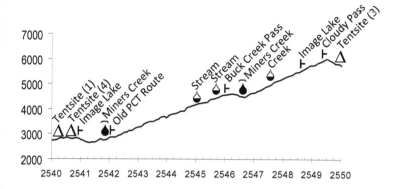

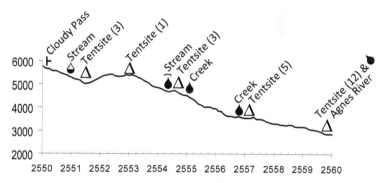

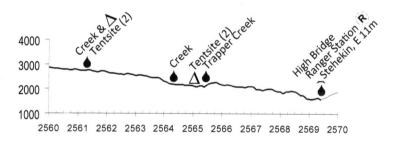

Skykomish to Stehekin

Skykomish   Mile 2462 W 14m   Population: 205

U.S. Post Office, 360-677-2241, M-F 11:30-3:30
Skykomish, WA 98288

Check out the Dinsmores at www.dinsmoreshikerhaven.com

Tip: Cascadia Inn offers affordable lodging and has a nice cafe.

Leavenworth   Mile 2462 E 37m   Population: 1,992

U.S. Post Office, US Mail, 509-548-7212, M-F 9-5 & Sa 9-11
Leavenworth, WA 98826

Tip: Leavenworth is styled as a Bavarian Village and is overrun with tourists.

Stehekin   Mile 2569 E 11m   Population: 75

U.S. Post Office, 509-682-2625, M,W&F 8-12 & 1:30-4:30, T&Th 9-3
Stehekin, WA 98852

Tip: The bakery here is amazing.

Cost Saving Tip: The campground located in Stehekin is an affordable alternative to staying in the lodge.

Stehekin to Canada

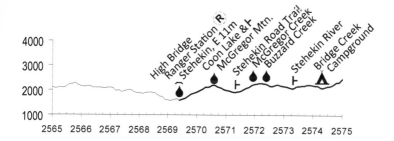

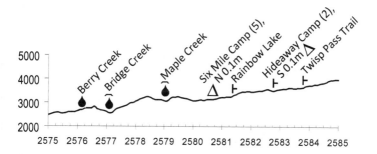

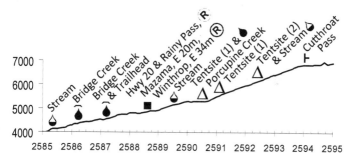

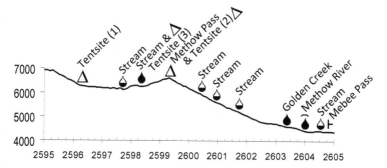

Stehekin to Canada

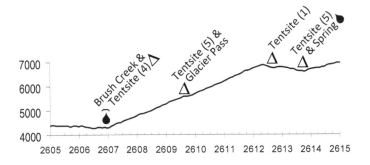

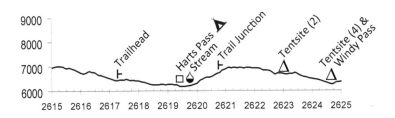

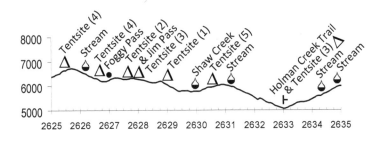

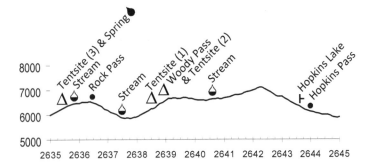

Stehekin to Canada

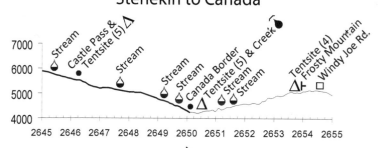

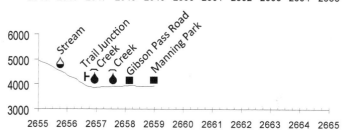

Stehekin Mile 2569 E 11m Population: 75

U.S. Post Office, 509-682-2625, M,W&F 8-12 & 1:30-4:30,
T&Th 9-3
Stehekin, WA 98852

Tip: The Bakery here is amazing.

Mazama Mile 2589 E 20m Population: 200

509-996-2515, Open Daily 9-5
c/o Goats Beard Mountain Supply
50 Lost River Rd.
Mazama, WA 98833

Tip: The Mazama Store has groceries and a deli.

Winthrop Mile 2589 E 34m Population: 415

U.S. Post Office, 509-996-2282, M-F 9-4:30,
Winthrop, WA 98862

Tip: North Cascades Mountain Hostel is friendly to PCT
hikers (northcascadesmountainhostel.com).

CHECK POCKETPCT.COM FOR UPDATES

Manning Park Resort

800-330-3321, Call for specific mailing instructions
manningpark.com
7500 Hwy #3, Manning Park, BC V0X 1R0

Tip: The lodge has a hot tub, sauna, steam room, pool, restaurant and across the street is a hostel.

Cost Saving Tip: A Greyhound bus stops at the Manning Park Resort once per day en route to Vancouver. Vancouver offers a wide variety of transportation options including bus, train and plane. Amtrak (train services) operates in Vancouver and provides affordable transportation to the United States.

Resupply Points

Stehekin
Skykomish
Snoqualmie Pass
White Pass
Washington

Cascade Locks
Timberline Lodge
Elk Lake Resort
Shelter Cove
Crater Lake
Ashland
Oregon

Seiad Valley
Burney Falls
Castella
Old Station
Belden
Sierra City
Echo lake
Tuolumne Meadows
Lake Edison
California
Kennedy Meadows
Tehachapi
Agua Dulce
Wrightwood
Big Bear City
Idyllwild
Warner Springs
Mt. Laguna

Pacific Crest Trail
2650 miles

Resupply Information

Popular resupply points along the PCT are provided in this book. To mail a package to a post office, use the general address below.

Your Name Here
c/o General Delivery
City, State   Zip Code

To mail a package to all other locations, follow the example below.

Your Name Here
c/o Name of Business
Street Address
City, State   Zip Code

In the lower corner of each side of the package, write your last name, "Hold for PCT Hiker" and "ETA: [month and day]" (ETA = Estimated Time of Arrival). Properly labeling the sides of your parcel makes it easier to locate your package.

Always independently verify the proper mailing address and delivery requirements prior to sending your parcel. Mailing addresses or requirements may change without notice. Visit usps.com or call 1-800-ASK-USPS for current post office information.

The resupply points along the PCT are indicated by a mile marker. The mile marker is followed by directions to the resupply point.

Always Independently Verify Mailing Information

Pocket PCT & Guthook's Guides
have teamed up to bring you

Guthook's Guide to the PCT

iPhone

Android

Our Customers Speak For Us:

"Kudos all the way around."

"I cannot say enough about this series of apps."

"Hands down the best choice for hiking the PCT."

"Looks great, intuitive and lots of excellent trail info."

Available in iTunes App Store
& Google Play Store

www.sierraattitude.com

Made in the USA
San Bernardino, CA
08 July 2020

75215772R00066